THE STRATEGIC ENEMY

THE STRATEGIC ENEMY

HOW TO BUILD & POSITION A BRAND WORTH FIGHTING FOR

LAURA RIES

WILEY

Copyright © 2025 by John Wiley & Sons. All rights reserved, including rights for text and data mining and training of artificial intelligence technologies or similar technologies.

Published by John Wiley & Sons, Inc., Hoboken, New Jersey.
Published simultaneously in Canada.

No part of this publication may be reproduced, stored in a retrieval system, or transmitted in any form or by any means, electronic, mechanical, photocopying, recording, scanning, or otherwise, except as permitted under Section 107 or 108 of the 1976 United States Copyright Act, without either the prior written permission of the Publisher, or authorization through payment of the appropriate per-copy fee to the Copyright Clearance Center, Inc., 222 Rosewood Drive, Danvers, MA 01923, (978) 750-8400, fax (978) 750-4470, or on the web at www.copyright.com. Requests to the Publisher for permission should be addressed to the Permissions Department, John Wiley & Sons, Inc., 111 River Street, Hoboken, NJ 07030, (201) 748-6011, fax (201) 748-6008, or online at http://www.wiley.com/go/permission.

The manufacturer's authorized representative according to the EU General Product Safety Regulation is Wiley-VCH GmbH, Boschstr. 12, 69469 Weinheim, Germany, e-mail: Product_Safety@wiley.com.

Trademarks: Wiley and the Wiley logo are trademarks or registered trademarks of John Wiley & Sons, Inc. and/or its affiliates in the United States and other countries and may not be used without written permission. All other trademarks are the property of their respective owners. John Wiley & Sons, Inc. is not associated with any product or vendor mentioned in this book.

Limit of Liability/Disclaimer of Warranty: While the publisher and author have used their best efforts in preparing this book, they make no representations or warranties with respect to the accuracy or completeness of the contents of this book and specifically disclaim any implied warranties of merchantability or fitness for a particular purpose. No warranty may be created or extended by sales representatives or written sales materials. The advice and strategies contained herein may not be suitable for your situation. You should consult with a professional where appropriate. Further, readers should be aware that websites listed in this work may have changed or disappeared between when this work was written and when it is read. Neither the publisher nor authors shall be liable for any loss of profit or any other commercial damages, including but not limited to special, incidental, consequential, or other damages.

For general information on our other products and services or for technical support, please contact our Customer Care Department within the United States at (800) 762-2974, outside the United States at (317) 572-3993 or fax (317) 572-4002.

Wiley also publishes its books in a variety of electronic formats. Some content that appears in print may not be available in electronic formats. For more information about Wiley products, visit our web site at www.wiley.com.

Library of Congress Cataloging-in-Publication Data is Available:

ISBN 9781394323937 (Cloth)
ISBN 9781394323944 (ePub)
ISBN 9781394323951 (ePDF)

Cover Design: Wiley
Cover Images: © eNJoy Istyle/stock.adobe.com, © AlenKadr/stock.adobe.com, © Philipp/stock.adobe.com
Author Photo: Courtesy of Mary Jane Starke
Illustrations: Laura Ries & Edward Sun

SKY10123036_073125

To Scott, my husband and strategic partner in life.

Together we have built a love worth fighting for.

Contents

	Preface	*ix*
	Introduction	*xi*
1	**The Mind Is Not a Computer**	1
2	**The Category Folders in the Mind**	15
3	**The Strategic Enemy**	29
4	**Don't Be Your Own Worst Enemy**	45
5	**The Power of Saying No**	65
6	**When You Focus, the Enemy Is Clear**	79
7	**An Enemy Fuels Debate**	103
8	**Wielding a Visual Hammer**	125
9	**Nvidia: A Positioning Success Story**	147
10	**Leadership Is Your Anchor**	163
11	**Giving Birth to Your Own Enemy**	175
12	**Getting Started: Strategy in Action**	191
	Notes	*199*
	Acknowledgments	*207*
	About the Author	*211*
	Index	*213*

Preface

In 1981, my father, Al Ries, and Jack Trout published *Positioning: The Battle for Your Mind*. It has become one of the most important, influential, and successful marketing books ever written.

The idea for positioning was simple, bold, and revolutionary. But where did it come from, and how did it become so famous?

In 1963, my dad founded a B-to-B advertising agency, Ries Cappiello Colwell, in New York City. As a small agency in the shadows of giants, it was hard to get noticed. To make a name for itself, they needed a different approach for the agency and its clients.

At the time, most advertising promoted claims. We are the best this or that. Everything was new, improved, better, and the best. What is the problem with saying you are awesome in your advertising? Nobody believes it. What you say about yourself is highly suspect and rarely believed.

The solution was simple. My dad's idea was to build every advertisement around what he called a "rock," an idea that differentiated the brand and that the prospect couldn't dispute.

When his agency developed a campaign for Uniroyal, they could have said, "Uniroyal makes the best rubber on the road." Puffery.

Instead, they communicated that idea in a much more believable way with the headline "Uniroyal holds more patents than any other rubber company." Best is subjective, the number of patents is a fact.

The mind rejects what isn't believable. An undisputable rock is more likely to be accepted into the mind.

Jack suggested that instead of a "rock" they should call the idea a *position*. My dad loved it. It had the advantage of suggesting brands own a "position in the mind." And the concept itself could be called *positioning*.

As with most brands, there was also a bit of luck involved in its success. For positioning, that luck involved my dad giving a speech that Rance Crain, owner and publisher of *Advertising Age*, attended. Rance was so impressed with the speech and concept that he invited Al and Jack to write a series of articles on positioning for the magazine.

In 1972 *Advertising Age* ran their three-part series titled "The Positioning Era Cometh." The basic premise of positioning was this: Brands should try to occupy a specific "position" in the mind of consumers. But that wasn't all they said.

They also took a very strong stance against creativity, not so much because they were opposed to it but because they wanted to establish a position in the mind for positioning. According to my dad, "You've got to knock out the enemy before you can occupy the position."

The articles set off the great marketing debate. At the time everyone believed communicating your idea with creative advertising was the linchpin to brand success. Positioning said brand strategy doesn't start with what you want to say; it starts with what the mind of the consumer is willing to believe and accept.

Positioning took off not just because it was a great concept but also because it repositioned the enemy it called *creativity*. Your brand needs to do the same.

Introduction

Positioning first rocked the world more than 50 years ago. If you are like me, you grew up with positioning. While the world has changed dramatically, the mind of the consumer has not. Positioning is based on the principles of how the mind works. It is still as relevant today as it was 50 years ago. Perhaps even more so.

Positioning plays a vital role in a company's success. Brands are the key drivers of valuation. Using positioning to decide the brand name, focus, category, visual hammer, and strategic enemy is essential. Positioning is also too important to be left to the marketing department; the CEO must captain the positioning strategy. Decisions on expansion, when to say no, when to launch new brands, and what to focus on for the future must come from the top. Nvidia is a classic positioning success case and a whole chapter of this book.

I often get asked if positioning strategies work for business-to-business (B2B) companies. Of course they do. In the business world, the brands you choose are critical, and your job is riding on it. That's why we say nobody ever got fired for buying from IBM. Today, it is more like nobody ever got fired for buying from Salesforce, Nvidia, or Microsoft, right? Buying from a company that has a strong brand and dominates the category is always seen as the safe choice.

The reason this book focuses on consumer examples is that more people have heard of these brands, and they are quicker to explain. This book is about strategies; the examples only illustrate them. Studying cases is the best way to learn and practice positioning.

Remember, marketing is not like physics. One outlier example doesn't prove the whole theory is wrong. Marketing is an art as much as it is a science. Each case is unique, and we have studied thousands of brands. When correctly executed, using positioning, focus, the strategic enemy, and a visual hammer will win out almost every time.

This book is full of great brands that started off with the enemy in mind. Take Liquid Death, one of the most successful new water brands. Identifying the enemy was an essential part of the branding process. Liquid Death's enemy is plastic bottles, so they launched a water brand in cans. Now they have a great name and killer marketing too. But would the brand be as successful if it was sold in plastic bottles? I think not.

Or go back in history. How would you best position a bus company? Better seats, better pricing, better routes? All nice to have, but Greyhound specifically called out an enemy: driving yourself. "Go Greyhound—and leave the driving to us." A slogan that rallied the brand for decades.

Positioning your brand against a strategic enemy makes your brand sharper and more memorable and unites people to your cause. Yet most companies continue to focus on "being better" and "expanding the brand" rather than on what really matters: being different. Using an indisputable difference and the distinctiveness of a visual hammer to drive your brand into the mind of consumers is what finding your strategic enemy is all about.

So, buckle up. This book will show you how finding a strategic enemy will make your brand something worth fighting for.

THE STRATEGIC ENEMY

Chapter 1

The Mind Is Not a Computer

The ultimate goal of branding is to position your brand in the mind of the consumer. The mind is like a computer memory bank with one important difference: a computer must accept what you put into it; a mind does not. In fact, the human mind is selective and will reject any information it determines doesn't compute. That's why changing a firmly held belief is so difficult and why contrasting a new idea to something already accepted is more effective.

■ ■ ■

The concept of positioning has been around for decades, and while simple in theory, applying it in practice is difficult. That's why I wrote this book, because identifying the strategic enemy is one of the most powerful tools in our positioning toolbox. While most leaders can name their brand's competitors in the marketplace, few can identify their strategic enemy. If this is you, you are not alone.

A strategic enemy is an oppositional force that your brand or category stands against. It could be a competitor, convention, or concept. Having a strategic enemy will force you to clearly define what you are not, which will enable consumers to more easily understand what you are.

While most brands have a positioning statement in a brand book, most are written to serve as an umbrella to cover everything they do. That's not positioning. Positioning is a strategy for dealing with the mind. Vagueness won't cut it; successful positioning strategies create clarity and contrast in the mind of the consumer. Positioning against a strategic enemy makes your position sharper and more memorable. It also energizes and motivates consumers to rally for your cause.

The human mind understands ideas best through contrast. The mind has always been the starting point of positioning, so I want to kick off this book with a quick review of how positioning is designed to deal with the complexities of the mind. The best way to explain this is to contrast how minds differ from computers. After all, if there is a strategic enemy of the human mind, it's the computer.

Computers are simple, predictable, and process whatever they are given. Many would like to believe the human brain functions in a similar way, as a straightforward input–output device that processes sensory data and then reaches a logical and well-thought-out conclusion. If this was the case, branding would be easy. You present your brand concept; consumers would process it and then decide whether to buy it or not.

Computers are ready and willing to process all inputs. Processing is how a computer thinks. And thinking requires an enormous amount of power for computers and people. As a result of artificial intelligence, computers today are hogging power like never before.

While we can feed computers more power to think, this is not the case with people. The world is demanding more and more from us just as AI is demanding more and more from computers. All of us are bombarded with too many message, too many brands, across too many media. The over-communicated society my father lamented over in the '70s and '80s has exploded to new heights in the twenty-first century.

So how do people cope? We constantly filter inputs and try to think as little as possible. Humans are cognitive misers compared to computers. To maintain our sanity, we have to carefully ration our thinking power, or we will burn out our brains.

Daniel Kahneman, the famed psychologist, made the perfect analogy: "Thinking is to humans as swimming is to cats. They can do it, but they'd prefer not to."

Too Many Choices

Making purchasing decisions today can be stressful due to the over-abundance of products, brands, and varieties available to consider and choose from.

A simple trip to your local supermarket will explain. The number of products, flavors, and size variations of brands that are on the shelves is outrageous.

Imagine you are asked to pick up some Gatorade. Sounds simple, until you get to the store and see the choices on the shelf. Of course, there are a multitude of flavors and size choices. But what really makes it particularly difficult are the line extension choices that all also carry the Gatorade or "G" name, such as Gatorade, G2, Gatorade Zero, Gatorade Fit, Gatorade Endurance, Gatorlyte, Fast Twitch by G, Gatorade Bolt24, and even Gatorade Water! Not to mention Gatorade protein bars. PepsiCo's online product search lists 557 entries for Gatorade products. How many Gatorades does the world really need? With all these line extensions there is little hope of finding a strategic enemy. Worse still, Gatorade has become its own worst enemy.

It's insane. Marketers incorrectly assume that more choices to choose from are what consumers want. Perhaps in research they may answer this way, but not in reality.

The famous jam experiment conducted by Sheena Iyengar and Mark Lepper in 2000 demonstrated that choice overload often leads to decision paralysis. In the experiment they set up a table at a supermarket and offered samples of a new jam to try. One table had 6 varieties of jam, and later they tested a table with 24 varieties. While people were initially attracted to the larger assortment, fewer people ultimately purchased any jam compared to when less options were displayed. Fewer choices ease the decision-making process and lead to more purchases.

Regardless of the choices, many consumers are on the hunt for the original most popular flavor and these additional varieties box it out from the shelf. I can't tell you how many times I have tried to find vanilla ice cream and can't. That one row is sold out and only the crazy concoctions are left.

Sadly, all this focus on increasing variety isn't necessarily increasing sales, and worse yet, coping with all these choices has become a hazard to our well-being.

In the book *The Paradox of Choice*, Barry Schwartz calls it the "Tyranny of Choice." He writes how having too many choices can be detrimental to one's health and happiness. Schwartz argues that overwhelming choices result in decision-making paralysis, anxiety, perpetual stress, and even depression. I agree.

Places like Costco make choosing easier and more decisive. Buy it or not. Fewer items, fewer choices. An average supermarket carries up to 60,000 individual products, and a Wal-Mart Supercenter carries up to 150,000. Costco, on the other hand, has only 4,000 items, so no wonder shopping there is a joy. Limiting options to a more reasonable number can make buying way more fun.

One of the tenets of a free market and capitalism is access to choices and opportunities. However, there can be too much of even a good thing. The best way to help consumers cope is by making the selection of your brand as simple as possible. Making it too difficult can even undermine and potentially erode your brand's position and value in the mind.

Take Organic Triscuits. This is an idea that doesn't compute in the mind. Most consumers believe that Triscuits are a wholesome cracker.

Triscuits are the original healthy cracker launched in 1903 and baked with 100 percent whole grain wheat. Forget the fact that the 23 different flavors—such as balsamic vinegar and basil, four cheese and herb and dill, and sea salt and olive oil—present a mind-blowing number of flavor options. When you add the decision of organic or not, this is more than a flavor line extension; it can be an existential brand crisis.

This juxtaposition of regular versus organic on the shelf influences your overall perception of the original Triscuit product that accounts for most of the brand's sales. The consumer is left with two equally bad choices. Buy the Triscuits and feel bad that they are not organic. Or pay more for the organic and feel duped that the cracker you loved for years wasn't all that good. Some choice.

Triscuits, of course, will argue that organic is a growing trend they needed to jump on to stay relevant. Perhaps, but at what cost to the brand perception in the mind? A better direction is to improve the quality of Triscuits and make them all organic, clearly doubling down on the idea. Or launch a new organic cracker brand. Or just be proud of Triscuits as a healthy choice as it is.

Changing a strongly held position is nearly impossible. Once a mind is made up, it's tough to budge. As the saying goes: "Don't confuse me with the facts, my mind is made up." Being wrong is something few people tolerate being told, especially with your marketing message. Seeing Organic Triscuits on the shelf makes you feel wrong about your previous view of the brand.

The Mind and Distinctiveness: The Power of Being Different

If consumers are limiting their thinking power and constantly looking to filter out information, how in the world will we get them to learn about our brand? After all, marketing messages are one of the first thing people openly beg to have less of in their lives unless it is Super Bowl Sunday.

It may seem obvious but being distinctive and different is a great way to attract attention. Yet what do most brands do? They launch copy-cat products that are neither distinctive nor different.

After the success of Red Bull, more than a thousand energy drinks flooded the market. All in 8.3 oz. cans. But not Monster. Every new brand knew the enemy was Red Bull, but Monster did something about it. Monster was different and distinctive by launching its energy drink in 16 oz. cans.

Too many companies focus all their energy on being better. Better products, better service, better prices. Yet when you tell consumers you are better, the mind treats that information as suspect. If you are cheaper, you certainly can't be better. And if you really were better, wouldn't you be the leader? Hard to argue with that logic.

When you tell consumers you are different, it begs the question: Why? Why are you different, and how does that make your brand better? It is more involving, creates news value, and opens the discussion. When you communicate that difference by also being visually distinctive, it is a powerful combination that solidifies the brand position in the mind.

So you might be thinking that today all energy drinks are available in 16 oz. cans. Monster is not different anymore, so why did it matter? True. Monster isn't different anymore, but being different got the brand into the mind of the consumer. Being different got our attention, and being in a bigger can was the basis for the name and strategy.

There are two challenges when building a brand. The first and biggest challenge (the Everest of challenges) is getting into the mind in the first place. This takes an enormous amount of effort. Pioneering a new category and/or being different are your sources of power. It's the plane getting off the runway using 110 percent of its power.

Once your brand is established in the mind, the challenge changes. Now you must reinforce the brand. Maintaining consistency is vital. Shoddy brand construction and poor pilots are a concern. Success will depend on how well your plane is built, branded, and navigates the horizon. You need to fly steadily and not hit any mountains.

Copycats will likely imitate your initial difference, but if your brand was first in the mind, it will be perceived as the original and the real thing—unless you hinder yourself with poor marketing.

We didn't say being different is enough. Marketing, not just innovation, is essential.

Monster built the brand by being different; today it remains uniquely distinctive with a great name (Monster), powerful visual hammer (the green claw), slogan ("Unleash the beast"), and extreme events, especially motorsports (Monster Truck Jam, Monster Supercross). Monster is a fierce number-two brand to Red Bull globally.

The Mind and Simplicity: The Power of the Oversimplified Message

Computers accept any information you enter as long as you remember to click "save." You can be long-winded, verbose, and even make spelling errors. Computers have vast computing power to deal with it, sort it, store it, and even auto-correct your bad spelling, for which I am forever grateful.

To make it into the human mind and get saved, the message itself is critical to craft. The most important aspect is oversimplification. It is a key tenet of positioning and one that many companies hate to embrace. Most companies want to communicate too many ideas and tell a story. The more detailed our story the better, right? Not necessarily.

There is nothing wrong with having a brand story. In fact, every brand needs one. The problem is getting people to stop and pay attention to it. The whole story is great for your PR, avid customers, and employees, but for the rest of us, oversimplification is the sharp knife tip that makes the first cut.

You need a sharp message that is simple and specific, verbalized in a memorable way. Then repeat it, repeat it, repeat it. An oversimplified message will become even more meaningful over time. It is the battle cry for the brand. Some great examples:

- Kit Kat: Have a Break, Have a Kit Kat. Since 1957.
- BMW: The Ultimate Driving Machine. Since 1974.
- Nike: Just Do It. Since 1988.

- Target: Expect More. Pay Less. Since 1994.
- Skittles: Taste the Rainbow. Since 1994.
- Dunkin' Donuts: America Runs on Dunkin'. Since 2006.
- Tommy John: No Adjustment Needed. Since 2015.

Dunkin' Donuts (now just Dunkin') has been using the slogan "America Runs on Dunkin'" since 2006. This simple slogan nails the difference between Dunkin' and Starbucks. Dunkin' is the brand that fuels everyday Americans who work hard. Using the nickname Dunkin' here was brilliant and the slogan hammers the coffee idea. We all know Dunkin' coffee is what fuels us. The donuts are optional.

Good slogans get even better with time. Nothing beats a simple message that reinforces your positioning. But honestly, they didn't need to drop "Donuts" from the name. The success of the slogan may have gone to their head. They ditched the memorable alliteration which leaves the name incomplete. Why are they running from donuts?

They should study what happened at KFC. In 1991, after almost four decades as a leading brand, Kentucky Fried Chicken changed its name to KFC. Why? Mainly they wanted to distance themselves from the unhealthy connotations of "fried." So, they shortened the name to the already popular nickname for the brand. Did that work? Nope. KFC could never escape its fried chicken perception in the mind, no matter what they changed the name to. The initials are simply an abbreviation for the spelled-out name. Most of us see KFC and know it stands for Kentucky Fried Chicken.

Short term the name change was fine for KFC, but now more than 30 years later, the younger generation sees KFC and they aren't so sure what the letters stand for. They don't have the memories of the original brand name. There is a benefit to keeping the full name that holds your history and allows customers to decide to use the nickname.

Luckily despite the name change, the brand's memorable "finger lickin' good" message has been consistent since 1956. And today "crispy" aka fried chicken is hot again.

Don't mistake brevity with oversimplification. The letters KFC are not a simplification of the name Kentucky Fried Chicken. KFC are meaningless letters to a new consumer that has never heard of them. And each year new consumers are born.

Kentucky Fried Chicken communicates an idea to new customers and reinforces the brand with existing ones. They obviously have realized this because they are moving back in this direction. Newly redesigned stores have the full spelled-out name on walls and interiors. Good move. The full name is authentic. Initials alone lack the emotional impact of saying Kentucky Fried Chicken and owning it.

The Mind and Brand Names: The Power of Being Specific

Powerful brands are built with a narrow focus. When you have a narrow focus a specific, distinctive name is easier to find. When your name includes words that can be visualized it makes it even more memorable. Specific names win out over generic ones in the mind. Even if you add a few more things to sell, it doesn't mean you need to sacrifice your specific name to do so. Yet, many companies believe they need to generalize their name if they expand the business.

In the early 1990s Boston Chicken was riding high as the rotisserie chicken king. They focused on rotisserie chicken as the healthier alternative to the enemy, fried chicken. (The rise of Boston Chicken was one of the reasons KFC became so concerned over its fried position.) Boston Chicken went public with great fanfare in 1993 with the hottest public offering of the year, but their success in chicken didn't satisfy them. Not only did Boston Chicken expand the menu with items like meatloaf, roast turkey, and ham, but they also changed the name from the specific Boston Chicken to the generic Boston Market promoting homestyle meals.

Five years later Boston Market filed for bankruptcy. What if they had stuck to the chicken name and focused on rotisserie? When you see or hear the name Boston Chicken, you visualize rotisserie in your mind. When you see or hear the name Boston Market, what is the visual? Specific names are more visual, memorable, and emotional.

The Mind Is Not a Computer

In 2009, Pizza Hut started promoting itself as The Hut. Removing pizza from the name signaled their intent on making The Hut the place for all types of Italian food. The potential name change was part of a diversification strategy that included a widely expanded menu. You know management sat around and said, "Pizza is too narrow; to grow we need to sell more stuff, and to sell more stuff we need a more general name. Let's drop pizza from the name and be The Hut." Too often so-called simplifications are all for the sake of expansion. Consumers, however, weren't buying it and they brought back pizza to the name.

Recently, Edible Arrangements shortened its name to Edible. Founded in 1999, Edible Arrangements pioneered sending edible fruit arrangements instead of flowers. The enemy was flowers. Why buy something that will die, when you can buy a delicious fruit arrangement you can eat? It was a hit and currently has more than 1,200 locations worldwide.

But they wanted to add more products including cakes, fruit platters, and—would you believe—flowers? So, they dropped the Arrangements from the name. Honestly, is there a brand rule I don't know about that says you can only sell it if it is in your name? Boston Chicken could have kept the name and sold a few meatloaf meals. And Edible Arrangements selling a few fruit platters and cakes is unlikely to confuse anybody. Not to mention, Edible on its own has a very different connotation. I can imagine there are some very disappointed customers who walk into their stores and see only watermelon cubes and no weed.

Less is not always more. Dropping key elements for the sake of brevity can weaken a brand name. Standing for something specific is best. Edible Arrangements was a clear name with an enemy. Edible on its own is not. And you can still sell fruit platters and cakes if your name is Edible Arrangements. I won't report you.

The Mind and Emotions: The Power of the Visual

Visuals matter. Computers don't get emotional. They process the input of words and visuals the same. Not so with the human mind.

Visuals connect to emotions in a way that words cannot. When you find a visual that communicates your words, you have a visual hammer that hammers your verbal idea into the mind.

Consider these visual hammers:

- Coca-Cola and the contour bottle—communicates Coke is the real thing
- McDonald's and the golden arches—communicates leadership
- Corona and the lime in the top of the bottle—communicates Corona is an authentic Mexican beer
- Tropicana and the straw and orange—communicates Tropicana is made from oranges, not concentrate
- Target and the target logo—communicates the name of the store

The meaning of some visual hammers is clear. Coca-Cola's bottle was the original and distinctive package. While rarely sold in glass bottles today, the bottle is a visual reminder of their authenticity as the real thing. When your brand name lends itself to a visual like Target, it is wise to visualize it. Even if your visual hammer simply communicates your brand name, it is a powerful emotional tool. If your brand is a pioneer and leader of a category, you have the opportunity to create a distinctive visual that communicates your leadership. The power isn't in the design of the golden arches; the power comes from knowing that visual belongs to McDonald's, the leading chain.

The Mind and Memory: The Power of Repetition

Brands need an oversimplified message that is memorable, emotional, and can be visualized, and then it should be repeated over and over again. Repetition is needed to make ideas more memorable and stick in the mind. A computer doesn't need repetition. A human mind does.

Repetition of a message also has the psychological effect of making ideas more believable. Why? The more often we hear a message, the more likely we are to accept it as true.

The tragedy is that most brands tinker and change their message and positioning so often that the words never get the chance to take hold in the mind.

One reason is that the brain craves the dopamine rush that encountering new ideas generates. A study published in *Neuron* found that dopaminergic novelty processing (a fancy way of saying your brain lights up when you encounter something new) makes a new idea hard to resist.[1]

This is great news for brands that are the pioneers of new categories. But this is terrible news for brands that continue to tinker with messages looking for a new rush.

If you are the brand owner, it can be incredibly neurologically boring using the same strategy year after year. Plus, many people will constantly entice you to change things up. Your CMO will want to make his or her career mark by launching a new positioning strategy. Your creative agency will want to pitch fresh ideas and a new campaign—and if you have just hired a new agency using the slogan of the previous agency isn't likely to fly. Agencies want to showcase and get credit for their own new ideas.

While it might be boring, using the same message for decades is more effective. For nearly 50 years, Ace Hardware has been repeating that it is "the helpful place." As a result, most people think it is. The "Ace is the place with the helpful hardware man" jingle first started in the 1970s. Now, of course, they use the more inclusive term "helpful folks" in the song. Employees wear shirts with the slogan to further reinforce the message. The concept of enclothed cognition suggests that clothing can influence our psychological state and behavior. When you wear a shirt that says you are helpful, it creates a psychological effect that makes you feel and act more helpfully.

In 2023, Ace ranked "Highest in Customer Satisfaction with Home Improvement Retail Stores" according to J.D. Power. It has ranked number one in 16 of the last 18 years. In 2024, they were second to Menards.

In 2025, Ace Hardware was recognized among the top 1 percent of all brands in *Forbes* Best Customer Service list of 3,500 companies. "To be recognized again by *Forbes* for our customer service is a tremendous honor and a true reflection of our dedication to customers," said Kim Lefko, CMO at Ace Hardware. "At Ace, helpfulness isn't just a slogan, it's a way of life. Our local store owners and red-vested-heroes go above and beyond to ensure our customers receive reliable advice and quality products for their projects."[2]

The Mind and Reality: The Power of Perception

Reality doesn't matter. Only perception does. Perception is reality in the minds of consumers. It's not just what your brand is—it's what people believe it is that defines its value and influence.

Psychologists and marketers know this well. If we believe something will be good, it will be. When we think it will be bad, it will be bad. If we think it will work, it will—at least in our mind.

Now you can't have long-term success with crappy products that don't work or taste terrible. But some aspects of your brand are relative. Red Bull doesn't taste great, but as an energy drink, it doesn't have to compete on taste.

If you have a bad experience with a brand you love, you chalk it up to an unfortunate mistake. If you have a bad experience with a brand you hate, you think, "See I knew it all along, they suck."

Computers always deal with the reality of the data. The mind deals with perceptions that can defy the reality of the data. The actual reality of any situation is difficult for the mind to compute if it differs from a strongly held perception.

The essence of positioning is to accept the consumer's perceptions as reality.

> **Core Concepts: The Mind Is Not a Computer**
> - Computers compute everything; human minds are selective.
> - Computers handle complexity; minds need simplicity.
> - Computers follow logic; minds are influenced by emotions and visuals.
> - Computers get it the first time; minds need repetition, repetition, repetition.

Chapter 2

The Category Folders in the Mind

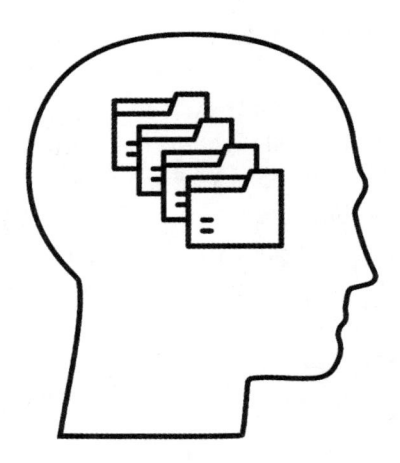

Understanding that brands are stored into category file folders the mind is the key to positioning success. The reality is that consumers have a hard time understanding what a brand stands for unless they first know the category it goes with. The greatest brand achievement is when your name can be used as a substitute for the category itself. If you use one name across multiple categories, you lose the opportunity to become the name replacement for a singular category. You also leave yourself vulnerable to a new brand that narrows the focus and makes you their strategic enemy.

■ ■ ■

People buy categories first; then they buy brands. Consider when you decide you want to buy a car. What do you think about first? The brand or the category?

The brand of car you ultimately buy is incredibly important to you. But is it the first thing you think about? Manufacturers would like to think so, which is why most offer a full line of vehicles to choose from. If consumers thought about the brand first, they would decide Ford, Toyota, or Tesla and then visit the showroom to see the different models available.

Of course, very few consumers think or act this way. They don't make brand decisions; they make category decisions first and foremost. The first decision any rational person thinks about is what category of vehicle to buy: car, truck, SVU, expensive car, cheap car, electric car, etc. Next people look into their minds to find what brand names they associate with that category.

The mind is not just haphazardly filled with information. It is organized into chunks of data that are stored and filed. The best analogy to represent this concept is file folders like what we use on a computer hard drive or in a file cabinet. Because categories are more important to consumers than brands, the names on the file folders are category names or positions. Not brand names.

When Consumers Change Categories

While it is true that many consumers buy their next car from the dealer that sold them the last one, this mainly holds true when they are sticking with the same category. Happy with your Ford F-150, you will return to your Ford dealer to get another one.

If consumers decide on a car from a different category, they will most likely consider and often change to a brand that better represents that category. For example, go from buying a cheap car to an expensive one. Or a SUV to sports car. Or a gas car to an electric.

Saturn was one of the most loved compact car brands in the 1990s. It was introduced by General Motors as "A different kind of car. A different kind of company." A new brand created to better compete with imports. Saturn's one model, one price, no haggle focus, called out traditional car dealers as the enemy. This rallied loyalty and love amongst consumers. They even hosted homecoming events where Saturn's owners went to the factory to celebrate where their car was born. At this time if you wanted a compact car, Saturn was likely a top pick. Or at least one of the showrooms you visited.

Then what happened? They expanded the Saturn brand into multiple category folders. Saturn launched expensive cars, sports cars, SUVs and more. The problem was when a Saturn owner got a raise and wanted a more expensive car, they also wanted a different brand that represented it, not a Saturn. And the loyal customers buying the basic sedans felt they were cheap instead of smart. Sales declined and in 2009 GM shut the brand down.

Dominating a category is the key to success. Too often companies are too quick to expand into new categories instead of continuing to build and expand the one they are in. Saturn should have stuck with its affordable and no haggle focus anchor.

Tesla pioneered the electric vehicle category as a new folder in the mind. To build a new category it is best done with a new brand that can call out the old category as the strategic enemy. Buying a Tesla is a statement against gasoline vehicles. Because Tesla dominates the category, any consumer switching to an electric vehicle will at least consider a Tesla. Many even buy one despite what they think of Elon Musk.

Creating a New Category Takes Patience

Categories rarely take off immediately; new ideas can take years to make it into the mind and then years more to result in significant sales. Being first in a new category means having the patience to build the category in the mind and then wait for the sales to come. It is another reason why spending big on advertising is the wrong way to build a brand. Advertising has no credibility, and worse still, you have no sales to support it. Tesla didn't use advertising, it used PR (public relations).

Go back to 2007, the year Tesla was founded. Suppose you asked the average car buyer in America that year, "What electric car might you buy?" The average buyer would say: "I have never heard of an electric car." That folder did not exist yet in the mind.

The nonexistence of the category back in 2007 is why most major auto manufacturers completely ignored the electric car market as a niche and didn't consider it worth their time nor investment. Patience isn't a virtue in most major corporations.

The numbers show just how long it took for the category sales to grow. By 2020, the electric-vehicle market represented only 2 percent of the total automobile market and Tesla dominated the category with 79 percent market share.[1] The power was not in the number of cars sold since it only sold 200,561 that year; it was in the supremacy of Tesla, owning the category in the mind of all car buyers. Virtually all the 14.6 million people who bought a different brand than Tesla that year knew that Tesla was the leading electric-vehicle brand. Tesla created the "electric-vehicle category" in the minds of almost all potential automobile buyers.

Being the dominant brand in the right file folder in the mind is the key to success. Tesla isn't a brand success story; it is a *category* success story. Tesla has benefited from more people checking out their EV file folder when deciding to buy a car.

In 2024, electric vehicles climbed to 8.1 percent of new car sales, and Tesla's market share declined to 49 percent; however, its dominance has not been diminished. General Motors and Hyundai are growing sales, but each represent only 12.6 and 11.4 market share, respectively.[2] Hot categories will attract competition. In a growing market it is most important to maintain your leadership position in the mind to maintain dominance of your category file folder.

A New Category Deserves a New Brand Name

When new technologies like electric cars emerge, there is an opportunity to launch new brands. Brands that exclusively focus on the new technology have the advantage of making the old technology their enemy. Brands that expand their existing name to the new technology expose themselves to risk if attacked by a narrowly focused new enemy.

Eveready created the battery folder in the mind. Founded in 1898, they invented the first electric hand torch (which later was renamed a flashlight) consisting of a dry-cell battery and a brass reflector inside a paper tube. As a result, Eveready dominated the battery category for decades when flashlights were the principal application.

In the late 1950s, new technologies such as transistors emerged which required more powerful batteries. Flashlight batteries were insufficient for these new tape recorders and radios. Alkaline batteries were introduced which were more powerful and longer lasting.

Naturally, Eveready expanded into this new alkaline category. They figured they had the best name in batteries, so they used the Eveready brand name. But they didn't have the best name in batteries, they had the best name in flashlight batteries.

The P.R. Mallory Company made batteries mainly for military equipment. They took advantage of this new alkaline battery category and launched a new brand with a great name, Duracell. Duracell, with its distinctive Coppertop went on to dominate the category and became synonymous with alkaline.

My dad wrote about this case history in *Positioning*. Shortly after the book was published, he called up Eveready's advertising manager and told him that they should introduce an alkaline battery with a new name. "We will never introduce a battery without the Eveready name" was his response. But they had no choice; Duracell was killing them.

In 1980, Eveready finally launched a new alkaline-only brand called Energizer. On the package there was a tiny Eveready over the big Energizer name. My dad liked to think it was a dig at him—the battery still had the Eveready name on it like the advertising manager promised. Too bad they didn't do it earlier. Duracell remains the leader and Energizer is number two.

The Importance of the Category Name

Creating a new category and owning that folder in the mind is difficult but highly lucrative if you succeed. While the brand name is incredibly important in the end, deciding the category name first is critical. Your new category name should instantly set up who the strategic enemy is. In some cases, the new category is easy to name—electric cars or alkaline batteries, for example.

In other cases, the category isn't so straightforward, and picking the right category name is essential. In the end, if you cannot define the new category in simple, easy-to-understand terms it usually is destined for failure.

What's Zima?

Consider Zima, an alcoholic beverage brand introduced by Coors back in 1992. Zima was launched at the peak of the '90s clear craze that gave us brands like Clearly Canadian and line extensions like Crystal Pepsi, Tab Clear, and Miller Clear. The clear line extensions were clearly crazy. Clear as an attribute for a new brand wasn't necessarily a bad move. "Clear" communicates purity and health. Clearly Canadian was initially a huge success as a flavored sparkling mineral water. What eventually killed it was too much sugar. It looked healthy, but being clear didn't mean it was devoid of sugar and calories. As soon as consumers figured that out, sales plummeted.

But aside from clear, what the heck was Zima? Even Coors had difficulty telling us. In fact, they made fun of the confusion by running ads with the headline "What iz it?" Clearly if Coors could not figure that out, what hope did the rest of us have?

The press mostly called it a malt-alternative beverage—in other words, an alternative to beer, wine, or spirits. Not a very consumer friendly term. "Clear malt" was also tried. But when you say "malt," most people think beer, and Zima was clearly not beer. It was a lightly carbonated alcohol beverage with a slightly sweet lemon lime taste, a long description not a category name.

A lack of clarity of what Zima was negatively impacted the perception of the taste because you taste in your brain. What you can't understand doesn't usually taste very good. Typical consumer descriptions of Zima said it tasted like tonic water with antifreeze, icky beer, or flat Sprite.

When you don't understand something or expect it to be bad, it will be bad. My dad loved to tell his college fraternity story when they would tell blind folded pledges to eat a bowl of worms, which was just cold spaghetti. The result? They all threw up because in their minds they were eating worms.

Zima has tried many strategies and reformulations over the year such as Zima Gold, Zima XXX, higher alcohol, lower alcohol, and lower calories—all of which had little impact. Once a brand is labeled as a loser, it isn't easy to fix. Better to cut your losses and try again.

Today the malt-alternative category is the hottest trend in alcohol beverages. But not because consumers perceive malt-alternative as a category. What led to this success were new brands that created categories which were easy to understand like hard lemonade, hard tea, and hard seltzer. Simple category names that didn't try to invent the wheel but used the word "hard" to communicate the products contained alcohol. Taste is always relative. White Claw honestly doesn't necessarily taste all that great, but as a hard seltzer it isn't so bad.

What's a Newton?

Apple's Newton also faced a category folder name problem. Introduced in 1993, Apple hyped the Newton as a revolutionary futuristic new device called a personal digital assistant. It's main features included a touchscreen, wireless capabilities, and handwriting recognition for notetaking.

The problem was the Newton was a device looking for a job to do, not a product built to solve a problem. It had no strategic enemy it was positioned against to replace. Apple never clearly defined who it was built for or what it could do best. Worse still, it wasn't very good at the main feature they claimed made it revolutionary: handwriting recognition.

The inaccuracy and unreliability of the handwriting feature led to some very bad press. It was endlessly mocked and the punchline of jokes on *The Simpsons* and *Doonesbury*. The product, technology, and marketing were flawed. The device was buggy, clunky, with half-baked software all sold at a super-premium price point.

When Palm Computing, a subsidiary of U.S. Robotics, launched the PalmPilot in 1996, they did things differently. They focused on business users and launched a handheld wireless device positioned as a practical tool that could sync your contacts and schedule from your computer to the device. It worked well, was easy to use, and sold at a reasonable price. It also had a clear strategic enemy: paper-based planners. While the computer was gaining traction as a place to input your data, you couldn't take it with you. PalmPilot replaced the old category of paper calendar and address books.

PalmPilot was also a great name. A computer that fits your palm and pilots your schedule. Personal digital assistant was never a great category name, it was eventually shorted to PDA, but most consumers just used the brand name PalmPilot. It was the dominant brand and the cult hit product back in the day, all others were imitations.

Don't feel too bad for Apple. Steve Jobs quickly killed the Newton when he returned to the company in 1997, and the technology and lessons learned paved the way for Apple's most successful new category folder ever.

Repositioning the Enemy's Category

In the 2000s, Nokia was riding high as the world leader in cell phones. In 2008, Nokia had an unbelievable 40 percent of the world's cell phone device market. If you checked the cell phone folder in your mind back then, Nokia dominated it.

BlackBerry was also a strong player with a new folder it created called wireless email. Avid fans of the device such as President Barack Obama were so addicted to using it, they referred to it as their CrackBerry. But like facsimile or Wang word processing, it was a temporary bridge category that would soon be replaced by something more permanent.

The iPhone could have suffered the same fate as the Newton, except it didn't. Steve Jobs, riding the success of the iPod, the first hard-drive music player, wasn't going to let Apple make the same mistakes they made with the Newton. He knew it needed to be promoted with a simple category name that made the enemy clear.

The revolution of the iPhone is easy to see in retrospect, but it wasn't apparent to everybody at the time. My own father questioned its potential. How could a device claim to do everything: phone, email, Internet, photos, and more? To my dad, it sounded like the Swiss army knife of phones. A little bit of everything but not very good at anything. Of course, that wasn't true; it was very good as an Internet device.

BlackBerry's keyboard maintained an advantage for users typing emails or text messages. Apple made the decision to sacrifice having a keyboard on the iPhone and only included a large touchscreen. While certainly not better for typing long emails, the touchscreen was the key distinctive ingredient for making the iPhone the first handheld Internet device. But Internet devices would have been a terrible name for the category, even though several phones including the BlackBerry touted Internet connectivity.

Apple instead launched iPhone as the first smartphone. This perfect category name communicated to the world its difference as well as its enemy. If the iPhone was a smartphone with its touchscreen, Internet, and apps, then all other phones were dumb by comparison. It instantly repositioned Nokia as the dumb phone brand. It is interesting to note that iPhone launched in 2007, and 2008 was the peak of Nokia's dominance and most likely profits.

Sinking ships many times make lots of money before they go down like the Titanic. Bloated and arrogant, they fail to take seriously the focused competition and category divergence creeping up on them. Of course, Nokia and every manufacturer eventually launched their own smartphones, but iPhone was first, is the specialist, and today has 20 percent of the global market. Nokia has disappeared into obscurity. For Nokia to have taken a stand, they would have needed a second brand.

To get into a mind, it is best to connect your new category idea to what's already in the mind. As the Internet invaded our lives, "smart" was the word used frequently to indicate a device that had an Internet connection. Apple just applied it to the phone. And other brands did as well by creating new smart categories of everyday products such as Nest and smart thermostats or Ring and smart doorbells.

The Category Folders in the Mind

Brands: How Consumers Ultimately Verbalize Categories

You Google the Internet, DocuSign a contract, Photoshop your photos, Uber to the airport, Xerox a document, blow your nose with a Kleenex, cover your boo-boo with a Band-Aid, clean your ears with a Q-Tip, throw your friend a Frisbee, and unwind in a Jacuzzi.

While the category is king, the brand name is the crown that identifies it and the way consumers verbalize it. Eventually the category name is replaced by the leading brand that is representative of the entire category itself. So even if you pick the right category name, if your brand name is weak, it leaves you vulnerable to an attack by an enemy with a better name.

One mistake is making your brand name too generic. The brand name should be unique, distinctive, and memorable. It should be instantly stored in the mind with a capital letter. Categories, on the other hand, should be generic and lowercase. You need both and they need to be different.

Gimme a Lite?

Today, light beer dominates the beer market. You would think the company that started the revolution using one of the greatest slogans in history would be the winner, but it isn't. And it all came down to a weak generic name.

Gablinger's Diet Beer was the first low-calorie beer in the market; the problem was it never established the category in the mind. The chemistry was right, but the name and marketing weren't. It did not go far. Convincing people to give this new category a chance would take not just a superior product, but marketing know-how. The recipe finally ended up with the Miller Brewing Company in 1972. And the rest is history, albeit one littered with missed opportunities.

Miller relaunched the product simply as "Lite." They tried incredibly hard to set up Lite as a new separate brand and not a line extension. However, it failed in the mind as well as the courts. The mind works by ear, not by eye. Yet most companies evaluate names by looking at them, not by listening to them. On paper Lite is a cute way to create a brand name out of the attribute "light." However, to the ear, light and Lite are the same. The mind has a difficult time recognizing either as a brand name.

The success of Lite was inevitably followed by other brands of light beer on the market. As a result, Lite had a tough time as a name. Asking for a Lite at the bar eventually ended up with the bartender asking "a light what?" Miller had to increase the prominence of the Miller name and promote it as Lite beer from Miller. More than a mouthful.

What saved the day was some of the best marketing in history. To win over Joe Six-Pack, Lite was heavily advertised using masculine pro sports players with the slogan "Tastes Great! Less Filling!" *Advertising Age* magazine named it the eighth best advertising campaign of the twentieth century. I don't disagree. Everything was perfect except the name. This serious error would eventually cost them dearly.

When a category filled with line extensions goes to battle, who do you think will win? The leader. When Budweiser, the king of beers, launched Bud Light, it was over. Even the great advertising Lite continued to do didn't help; it only helped propel Bud Light further ahead.

Bud Light got so brazen that they ran "Gimme a light" ads poking fun at the ridiculous idea the Lite could be a brand name. Asking for a light was meaningless: "If you just ask for a light beer, you never know what you'll get. So, if you want the less filling light beer with the first name in taste, don't just ask for a light beer, ask them to bring out their best. Bud Light, cause everything else is just a light." It was a super offensive strategy, and Bud Light won the game.

What should Miller have done? Easy. They should have given the beer a new name. A name without diet, light, or Lite. A name like Coors could have worked wonders. Bud Light had the advantage against other line extensions, but not against another brand name that wasn't an extension.

Sadly, Coors missed the opportunity to be the first brand to stand for light beer. Coors could have made regular beer the enemy and strongly promoted the superiority of the light beer category.

The Category Folders in the Mind

In the mid-'70s my dad met with Coors management on three separate occasions. He begged them not to line extend the Coors brand by introducing Coors Light, which they were considering. Instead, he suggested they reposition the Coors brand as the pioneer in light beer. After all Coors Regular had fewer calories than Michelob Light. It was known locally as Colorado Kool-Aid, born for drinking in the Mile High City. Coors missing out on this opportunity drove my dad bonkers. Sure, Coors Light has had success, but it could have been far greater without being just another line extension.

Need a Lift?

Uber was the pioneer in ridesharing. Lyft was second. But the name is weak. When you are the second brand in a category, having a weak generic name is a killer. Lyft is a brand name created by the alternative spelling of a generic word. Again, the problem is the mind works by ear and this name was as confusing as Lite was in beer. Confusion with the generic category word leads to problems. It's not easily stored in the mind and can't be used in conversation. If someone asks you if you need a Lyft, most will answer no thanks I'll order an Uber.

Lyft tried to distinguish itself with quirky pink mustaches on its cars. The name and the mustache visual did little to help them build a strong brand, neither made sense, and they were impossible to file in the mind. Lyft needed a differentiating strategy that setup up Uber as the strategic enemy.

In the United States, Uber maintains 76 percent of the rideshare market compared to only 24 percent for Lyft. Going against a dominant brand needs more than a cute mustache, it needs a better name.

Fresh Pet Food?

Launched in 2006, Freshpet was the first fresh dog food brand, but the name is weak. It's too generic. Fresh pet food is the category; as a name it's not distinctive or unique enough to be a great brand name. The strategy was right, the name was not.

Freshpet went public in 2014 and had annual sales of nearly a billion dollars in 2024. Impressive. It demonstrates a strong interest in the category itself.

The rise of pet humanization where we treat our pets as people has resulted in consumers becoming more aware of the well-being, diet, toys, and wardrobe of their pets. In South Korea, dog strollers outsell baby strollers. When I was a kid, walking the dog required the dog to walk. Now, people walk, and the dog gets a ride. It's a good time to be a dog.

As a category takes off, however, even the pioneer will face tough competition, and unless your strategy and especially the name are right, you are vulnerable.

The Farmer's Dog launched in 2014 with a better name and more focused strategy. They sell subscription boxes of personalized fresh dog food directly to consumers. When you focus you have a better chance of finding a good brand name.

Most importantly, The Farmer's Dog clearly identified the enemy they call "brown burnt balls," also known as kibble. "Eating processed foods for every meal is bad for you, why would you feed this to your dog?" It is specific and strong. There are many benefits to fresh, but Farmer's Dog focuses on longevity with the slogan "Long Live Dogs." Eating processed food will shorten your dog's lifespan.

Freshpet probably did research that showed a negative perception that spending more on fresh food was spoiling your dog. So Freshpet ran ads like this one: Guy is cooking dinner for his date. The date opens his refrigerator and is appalled to find dog food in there next to the human food. Gross! The commercial ends with the date no longer there and the guy eating dinner on the floor with his dog. Slogan: "It's not dog food, it's food food." Who is the enemy, people who don't care about dogs?

The Farmer's Dog has been hammering the enemy and positioning themselves as the alternative to highly processed food which no human or dog should eat for every meal of their life. Hard to argue with that.

A 2023 Super Bowl ad for The Farmer's Dog featured a young girl through the years—adolescence, college, her wedding—as her labrador retriever aged. It was a compelling claim for dog owners: A diet of The Farmer's Dog will keep your furry dog friend alive longer.

While the company has kept its financial performance quiet, PitchBook estimates annualized net revenue at $1.2 billion.[3] That would put it ahead of the pioneer FreshPet.

Names matter. If somebody asks my husband if we feed our beloved poodle Cocopuff Freshpet, he will answer of course we buy The Farmer's Dog.

Sometimes new category ideas aren't that hard to spot. The Famer's Dog was a hit with fresh food for dogs, so how about fresh food for cats? In 2017, Smalls was launched. Smalls? Fresh food for cats is a great idea, but the name is weak. However, because of the narrow focus, they created a memorable longevity message for cats: "Make 9 lives 10." The problem remains, though. How to drive a weak brand name like Smalls into the mind? The ads which end with how your cat will love the box as much as the food are cute and spot on if you have ever owned a cat. You could never say that about dogs. Dogs could care less about a box. But I can also let our cat play with all my Amazon boxes, no Smalls needed.

> **Core Concepts: The Category Folders in the Mind**
> - Consumers think category first, brand second.
> - Categories are ultimately verbalized by the dominant brand.
> - Since consumers speak in brands, your brand name is critical.
> - Generic category names make weak brand names.

Chapter 3
The Strategic Enemy

When you define what you're against, it becomes clear what you are for. Instead of making claims your brand is better, it's better to contrast with a strategic enemy how your brand is different. The mind understands opposition faster than superiority. Positioning your brand against a strategic enemy elevates your brand from "just another choice" into the right choice. It forces your brand to sharpen its focus to become a brand worth fighting for. The enemy could be a competitor, but it could also be another category, convention, or concept.

■ ■ ■

Having a strategic enemy is not about hate. It is not about good versus evil. It is not about your brand being right and the enemy being wrong. The enemy is about acknowledging that the consumer is making a choice. Whether you like it or not. And setting up that choice so it is clear and simple to make.

Decisions, no matter how trivial, are rarely made in isolation or without considering alternative options. Yet most companies sit in boardrooms and on video calls and only talk about themselves. Discussing the enemy when it comes to marketing is gauche. Companies want to rise above comparisons and focus on themselves and the positive. Never put anybody down.

Positioning is about how your brand is perceived in the mind relative to competitors. Much has been written saying that being different no longer matters, only being distinctive does. I would argue you can't leverage being distinctive unless you first establish a difference.

Here is the bottom line: To build a brand, you need to be first in something by either pioneering a new category or narrowing your focus. If you look back in history, almost every successful brand story begins this way. They all focused and strongly positioned themselves against a clear strategic enemy.

- Colgate was the first toothpaste in a tube. Enemy: tooth powders.
- Tiffany was the first raised prong engagement ring. Enemy: bezel settings.
- Tide was the first heavy-duty synthetic detergent. Enemy: soap.
- Scope was the first good-tasting mouthwash. Enemy: medicine breath.
- Salesforce was the first CRM in the cloud. Enemy: software.
- Tropicana was the first orange juice sold not from concentrate. Enemy: frozen concentrate.

When the Leader is the Enemy

For brands in second place, the enemy is easy to define; it is the leader. Saying you are better than the leader won't work. The prospective customer thinks: If you were so much better, why are you not the leader? You need to find a way to turn the leader's weakness or lack of focus into your strength, setting up a choice between you and your enemy that favors you but still honors the leader's position. In other words, just saying the leader sucks isn't going to work.

The enemy of Pepsi is Coca-Cola. If Coca-Cola is the real thing, it has been around forever. In other words, your parents drank Coke. Pepsi positioned itself as different by being the choice of a new generation. Great strategy. What doesn't matter are the numbers. The average age of Coca-Cola and Pepsi drinkers is the same; what is different is how the brands are perceived in the mind.

The enemy of Target is Wal-Mart. If you think competing against Coca-Cola is hard, this one is a beast. But for every position, there is an alternative. While Wal-Mart has the advantage of low prices with its "everyday low price" position, they can't claim to be fashion forward. And believe me they have tried. The brand made its debut at New York Fashion Week in 2024 and is hosting a Walmart Style Tour. Unlikely to work. The mind will reject Wal-Mart as a fashion brand; the concept doesn't compute. Target successfully positioned itself against Wal-Mart as the fashionable mass retailer with its well-known nickname Tar-zhay, a faux-French pronunciation suggesting the cheap chic focus of the brand.

A brand in third place against two strong enemies is about the worst place to be. Kmart for example had no hope against Wal-Mart and Target. Your best option is to narrow the focus or reposition your brand so you can be perceived as being first in a new category.

Maev entered the fresh dog food category by narrowing its focus using a key indisputable difference: It is raw food compared to the leader, The Farmer's Dog, which is lightly cooked. Is raw better? Who knows? You don't build a brand better; you do it by being different.

Entrepreneurs are wise to not just identify the enemy but to publicly call them out. To build a brand, you need to rally employees, investors, consumers, and the media to your cause. Nothing gets more attention than a battle between brands, categories, or concepts.

The Strategic Enemy

When the Existing Category Is the Enemy

Every new category should position itself against an existing category by treating it as the enemy. If you can relate your new category name to the previous category name, even better. iPhone was the first smartphone. A brilliant new category name that instantly implied all other cellphones by comparison were dumb.

Sara Blakely launched Spanx as footless pantyhose. Today the brand is more commonly referred to as shapewear, but it didn't start that way. The footless pantyhose as a category name was easy to understand and made the strategic enemy clear.

When you say footless pantyhose, female consumers instantly understood exactly what the product was and why it makes sense. Nothing beats the feel of control top pantyhose, but the hose part was no longer desired.

Body-shaping undergarments from corsets to girdles have been around for centuries, but most led to unsightly bulges or panty lines. Spanx could have been launched as a "better" shaper, but footless pantyhose more clearly communicated the no-lines differentiator. Over time, consumers use the brand name, not the category name. You wear Spanx.

Uber (The Enemy: Taxis)

Calling out an enemy means to truly stand for something to your customers, employees, and the world. Solving a problem as a new business idea is one thing; establishing a new category and the clear enemy of it is another.

One winter night in Paris in 2008, Travis Kalanick and Garrett Camp couldn't get a cab after attending a conference together. It led to an epiphany: "What if you could request a ride from your phone?" The iPhone was barely a year old, so this was a very forward-thinking idea. Camp immediately bought the domain name UberCab.com. In 2010, they tested the idea in New York City with three cars. Then launched the business in San Francisco.[1]

Sometimes you are a marketing genius, sometimes it is luck or a lawsuit. No matter how it happens, the resulting success is yours to own. In October 2010, the San Francisco Metro Transit Authority and the California Public Utilities Commission sent UberCab a cease-and-desist order alleging that the name "UberCab" could mislead the public into thinking the service was a licensed taxi operation.

Not wanting to fight the city, the company simply dropped "Cab" from the name and became "Uber." It was a stroke of genius prompted by a process server. They could not claim cabs were the enemy with "cab" in their name. With Uber as the name, they could establish a new category that took on taxi cabs as the clear enemy. Names matter.

Liquid Death (The Enemy: Plastic Water Bottles)

Being different doesn't necessarily require product innovation. Take Liquid Death. The product itself is mundane. They are selling the same spring water that countless other companies sell. What drove Liquid Death's valuation to a billion dollars was the differentiated packaging and branding.

Mike Cessario, an advertising executive with an affinity for fitness, health, and punk rock, was frustrated that junk food marketing was having all the fun. The best creative ideas were being used to sell stuff to people that wasn't good for them while the healthier options were marketed in serious, boring, and humorless ways. Mike's big idea? Take something healthy and environmentally friendly and make it cool and even a bit scary.

We all know water is healthy. What is not healthy is the global environmental impact of the plastic bottles used to sell the water in. Eighty percent of water bottles made of plastic end up in landfills and take up to 1,000 years to decompose. It is an enormous problem that is well-known yet often ignored for convenience.

Mike wanted to do something to change that. His idea was to package water only in 100 percent recyclable aluminum cans to directly address the environmental issues linked to plastic bottles. Aluminum cans are infinitely recyclable. Roughly 75 percent of all the aluminum produced since it was first industrially refined in 1888 is still in use.[2]

Many people are eager to drink more water and less energy drinks and alcohol. In fact, Mike seeing rock band musicians at the

Vans Warped Tour music festival drinking water from sponsored energy drink cans on stage sparked his idea. What if water could be marketed with the same intensity as energy drinks?

And Liquid Death was born. A water brand with a shocking name sold in tallboy beer–like aluminum cans and that was promoted with all the outrageousness and insanity of a heavy-metal band.

The enemy: plastic. The promise: death to plastics. The branding is edgy and unconventional but the commitment to sustainability is serious. One without the other would not be as effective.

Being different paid off, and Liquid Death's rise has been meteoric. Sales grew from $3 million in 2019 to $110 million in 2022 to $333 million in 2024. Liquid Death is valued at $1.4 billion following its March 2024 funding round of $67 million.[3]

Dude Wipes (The Enemy: Toilet Paper)

Sean Riley, the "chief executive dude" of Dude Wipes, found the inspiration for his brand in college during a routine trip to the store.

"I was living with all my buddies in a big Animal House apartment, and I was responsible for buying some of the goods one week," says Sean. "I went to Sam's Club, got toilet paper, paper towels, and a bunch of baby wipes, and stocked the bathrooms. You have to remember, these are guys eating tons of burritos, drinking tons of beers like you're partying after college—there are lots of bathroom breaks being taken. The baby wipes just came in handy and everyone got hooked on them right away. That was kind of when the light bulb product moment went on."

Sean wondered, "Why are guys using baby wipes and loving them? Why isn't there anything else on the market? Why isn't there something flushable with cool branding?"[4]

There were plenty of options of flushable wipes for adults in the aisle, but they were all line extensions of traditional toilet paper brands. Kleenex Cottonelle FreshCare Flushable Cleaning Cloths was the first moist toilet tissue. Yes, that was the full name. A name only a big company would come up with! Launched in the early 2000s, the messaging promoted using these new flushable cloths along with Cottonelle toilet paper. It was dual-product approach aimed at promoting both dry and moist products together.

Soon after, Charmin responded with its own line of products called Charmin Freshmates. Like FreshCare, they were marketed as a complement to traditional toilet paper. Of course they were. This made sense for the company but not for the consumer. The line extension names and weak messaging didn't generate any excitement for the category. And it certainly didn't resonate with Sean and his buddies.

Flushable moist toilet paper is a revolutionary idea. As such, it is best established by contrasting it to a strategic enemy. This was the opportunity Dude Wipes took advantage of. They didn't invent the product, they just positioned it against an enemy "traditional toilet paper" using bold branding and clear positioning. Today, Dude Wipes is giving Kimberly-Clark and P&G a run for their money in the bathroom.

Dude Wipes took something many felt taboo talking about and made it cool. They also focused on men, not women. Toilet paper and baby wipes brands are primarily aimed at women. Dude Wipes did the opposite. Unlike women, men only use toilet paper when they go number two, making them ideal targets for the product. A man living alone can survive with Dude Wipes alone in the bathroom.

Then they hammered the strategic enemy. Dry toilet paper doesn't cut it. Send toilet paper back to the Stone Age. That isn't a tagline Charmin or Cottonelle could use, but it is the type of messaging needed to create and popularize a new category in the mind. The same way Duracell hammered its alkaline batteries lasted longer than Eveready's.

But what about women? Sean told me one of the most common questions he gets asked is when he plans to launch Lady Wipes. His answer: Never.[5] Smart strategic thinking. There is power in being focused. There is power in the name Dude Wipes. When ladies do a number two, they need the strength of a Dude Wipe to clean up. I have no doubt the brand will resonate with female buyers just as much as it does with men. I do Dude Wipes.

UNTUCKit (The Enemy: Tucked Shirts)

When Chris Riccobono attended an all-boys Catholic high school in Ramsey, New Jersey, wearing his uniform shirt untucked led to detention.

Today Riccobono is the leader and spokesperson of what is being called the Untucked Nation with the brand he co-founded in 2011, UNTUCKit.

Untucking wasn't new; men bucking the formality of the tuck had been on the rise. The *New York Times* reported back in 2004 on the growing number of businessmen and celebrities pulling out shirts from pants for a more casual look.

Riccobono seized on the trend; he was the first to design a shirt that looked best worn untucked and launched his brand to focus exclusively on it. It was not all smooth sailing; investors instantly pooh-poohed the idea. The older ones failed to understand the concept, and the younger ones thought it would never catch on. Worse still, they all hated the name. They told Chris a fashion brand required a sophisticated name. UNTUCKit was the opposite: unsophisticated and specific. Investors suggested calling it "The Chris Riccobono Shirt."

To build a brand you need to identify your enemy and then do as much as you can to be different. The Ralph Lauren shirt was the enemy. For UNTUCKit using a similar name would not have been distinctive at all. As a brand built to disrupt the status quo, being different was required.

Even though UNTUCKit is a rather generic name, you need to judge the name by the category it is in and competitors it faces. In fashion, personal names reign supreme: Calvin Klein, Tom Ford, Tommy Hilfiger, Ralph Lauren, Brooks Brothers. Not to mention Gucci, Prada, Dior, Canali, Ferragamo. The goal for the name was not to do the same but to be different. In this regard, UNTUCKit is a great name.

A visual hammer is essential for fashion brands, a simple visual to communicate and broadcast to the world what brand you are wearing. Ralph Lauren's Polo shirts had the polo player. A visual that communicated the high-end position for the brand. Polo isn't a cheap sport.

UNTUCKit's visual hammer is its triangle located on the bottom left hem of the shirt to signify that it is the original brand made to be worn untucked. The triangle which they call their "signature sail" has become iconic and is widely recognizable.

As of 2025, UNTUCKit has $200 million in sales and has expanded from e-commerce and opened more than 100 retail locations. Having a retail presence is a fantastic idea. It brings street visibility to the brand and clothing brands always benefit from allowing consumers to touch it and try it on in store.

While expansion into retail is a good idea, I am less thrilled about the brand's line extensions. Their product range now includes pants, sweaters, jackets and even a women's line. What really bothers me are the ladies' shirts they sell are to be worn tucked in. Why on Earth would they do that? It goes against the one strong idea that built the brand.

The enemy of UNTUCKit is tucked-in shirts. There are plenty more people who are not aware of UNTUCKit and are prospects for the brand. The company should stick to their focus and mantra of shirts designed to be worn untucked. Keep the battle cry consistent, like a drum beating. "We are the rebels against business uniform standards of tucking. We fight to live life untucked."

Dockers (The Enemy: Dress Pants)

Shakespeare's famous line "A rose by any other name would smell as sweet" too often leads companies to underestimate the power of using a new name over a line extension. Would Levi's khakis have sold as well as Dockers khakis? I doubt it. Same pants with a different name made one smell so much sweeter.

The decision to launch a new brand or not comes down to the category. If you expand into what will be or could be perceived as a new category then a new brand name is best. If you use one name on both categories (Levi's jeans and Levi's khakis) you become your own worst enemy. If you use a new name for the new category (Dockers) you give birth to your potential enemy, which isn't necessarily a bad thing. In fact, it can be a great strategy.

In 1986, Levi Strauss launched Dockers, which focused on khakis trousers, targeting professionals who were looking for a middle ground between formal and casual wear such as jeans. The enemy was formal business attire.

What Levi's did to promote Docker's is what solidified the brand and its category success. While workers wanted to dress more casually, companies had dress codes after all. Docker's needed the support of management to rally the cause.

In 1992, Dockers distributed its famous "Guide to Casual Businesswear" to more than 25,000 HR managers across the United States. The goal was to clearly define what business casual meant and provide tips on how to dress casually yet professionally with Dockers khakis featured as the ideal choice.

Next, they promoted Casual Fridays. This allowed companies to give business casual a chance. Companies hate to make radical changes. What's the harm in letting employees dress casually once a week? The campaign not only built the Dockers brand but redefined workplace fashion. In just a few short years Dockers became a billion-dollar brand, and casual dress became the de facto every day of the week.

While Dockers generated $1.4 billion in annual revenue in 2004, now over 20 years later it is a brand in trouble. Nothing is wrong with the brand, but the category it owns has faded. There isn't much Dockers can do about this. When your brand's category declines, your brand does too. Just ask Kodak.

Dockers is still a 300-million-dollar brand. They should maintain their anchor as the pioneer of business casual and hope for a rebound in dressing up again. Fashion tends to be cyclical. While Lululemon leggings for women and ABC pants for men are in vogue today, business causal could make a comeback. We all got lazy staying at home during the COVID pandemic in our pajama pants and a nice shirt for Zoom. Nobody sees your pants on a video call, and that was a problem for Dockers. As more workers are back at the office, however, pants are a must. And nice pants are a plus.

Vineyard Vines (The First Enemy: Boring Ties)

In 1998, Shep and Ian Murray were two brothers working tedious desk jobs in marketing and PR. Both were miserable so they decided to quit their jobs to become entrepreneurs and chase the American Dream. They just needed an idea.

If you had to pick a product to launch a new business at the turn of the twenty-first century, neckties seemed like an awful choice.

A strong trend toward more casual dress had been going on for decades. And the necktie was about the first thing most men were ditching.

Doing the opposite, however, is a great way to launch a brand. The Murrays also had a powerful thesis in support of their necktie focus: "Yes, guys were wearing ties less often, but when they did, they wanted to make a statement. And neckwear had high margins and no sizing issues."

The brothers now cheekily comment in interviews that they started making ties because they hated wearing them at their former desk jobs. While that may be true, ties were an intentional and wise choice. They are a key part of the classic look worn on Martha's Vineyard, where the brothers fondly spent summers. Shirts, ties, blazers, and Nantucket Red (a shade of red faded to resemble a salmon color) pants make up the preppy but not fussy look. While plenty of other brands were known for preppy shirts, pants, and jackets, what necktie brands can you name? None. It didn't mean it was a sure thing, but it gave them something to drop their brand anchor with. A narrow focus also makes finding a brand name easier. The name Vineyard Vines was perfect for neckties with the colorful and whimsical designs of Martha's Vineyard.

Vineyard Vines launched on a shoestring. The brothers ran up $8,000 in credit card debt and spent the summer of 1998 selling ties in the parking lots, beaches, and bars of Martha's Vineyard. They printed catalogs at Kinkos, placing the ties on the photocopier. Unable to afford models, they used friends. While today they can afford models, they continue the tradition of using friends.

They got lucky in 2002 when Aflac ordered 10,000 custom ties with the company's duck visual hammer for $400,000. They hustled to fill the order, bribing pals with pizza and beer, and the brand was on its way.

In 2004, they expanded beyond ties and in 2005 opened their first store on Martha's Vineyard, of course. They also added the whale logo, a brilliant visual hammer for the brand. The whale was an easy choice since it is the most recognized symbol of Martha's Vineyard. Pink, on the other hand, was a bold color choice for a menswear brand, but pink was different and authentic to the vibe of the island.

As of 2025, Vineyard Vines does half a billion in revenue and has more than 125 retail stores. In an age where other retailers are shuttering stores, Vineyard Vines continues to push aggressively into brick and mortar. They also shun mainstream chains and online resellers. While expansion into either of these would be a short-term windfall, it allows them to maintain the integrity and exclusivity of the brand and shopping experience.

Brands are built with a narrow focus, like Vineyard Vines and ties. It established their credibility and set the brand anchor in the mind. With a strong visual hammer, they expanded into all types of preppy clothing. Now they face a new strategic enemy, the original preppy brand with the polo pony.

Ralph Lauren (The First Enemy: Shirts with Pockets)

Vineyard Vines wasn't the first fashion brand to start with ties. Ralph Lauren got his start by launching a collection of wide, hand-made ties under the name Polo in 1967. But it was his shirts embroidered with the Polo Pony logo that made the brand and Ralph an icon.

Shirts that polo players wear is a pretty narrow focus, but the target isn't necessarily the same as the market. While the clothes were designed with aesthetics polo players preferred, the sporty yet luxurious style of Polo has much wider appeal.

The Oxford shirt really did come from Oxford University. A nineteenth-century Scottish fabric mill created fabrics named after Harvard, Cambridge, and Yale, but only the Oxford one endures thanks to its versatility, durability, and weave that gets better with time and wear. The shirt became a favorite of English polo players who pinned down the collars to keep them from flapping in their face during play. Pins eventually gave way to button down collars.

Polo's strategic enemy was traditional dress shirts with pockets. Ralph Lauren launched his Polo Oxford shirts with no chest pockets and buttoned-down collars. The notion of a man wearing a dress shirt with no chest pocket and a button-down collar was as crazy as wearing a shirt untucked. Today, this look is ubiquitous. But at the time it was a unique distinction that was connected to the brand's Polo player style. Polo leveraged this distinction and visual hammer to build a powerful worldwide brand.

Lalo (The Enemy: Ugly Plastic High Chairs)

There is nothing more exciting than awaiting the birth of your first child. As soon-to-be first-time parents, you are suddenly thrust into a whole new world of categories, brands, and decisions. Breastfeed or bottle feed, co-sleep or not, breast pumps, bottles, baby wearing, swaddling, car seats, strollers, monitors, and more.

Impending parenthood usually comes with lots of opinions of what you will and will never do. Bold declarations such as my living room will never be taken over by toys.

But as one of my favorite movies, *Reality Bites*, reminds us, your dreams and plans will soon face the harsh reality of life. No sooner than that baby gets home does your home usually resemble a war-torn Toys R Us. Mine certainly did.

Baby and toddler brand Lalo is helping millennial parents reclaim their minimalist aesthetic dreams. Lalo is focused on designing simple baby and toddler essentials in colors like coconut, sage, and blueberry that blend into the homes of modern parents.

Lalo's first product "The Daily," was a $715 stroller that had no clear enemy. Upending the stroller market with a sleek design wasn't new, it had already been done. Bugaboo was the first; it gained popularity and me as a customer in 2002 after the "Bugaboo Frog" was featured in an episode of *Sex and the City*. Lalo's "The Daily" was too late to the stroller game to make a big splash.

Many entrepreneurs don't get it right on the first try. These initial failures go unnoticed. We only remember the ultimate success, because it was the anchor that was dropped into our mind. So, if at first you don't succeed, make changes and try again.

Lalo's next product, called "The Chair," was the right product at the right time with a clear enemy in mind. Typical high chairs are home décor eyesores. These ugly, bulky, plastic monstrosities instantly delete any remaining coolness factor from your home. Lalo created the perfect product with a well-defined enemy to launch its attack.

Lalo's "The Chair" garnered enormous publicity and TikTok attention for its sleek, functional, and versatile design. It was ranked by *Forbes* as the "Best Highchair Overall."[6] What does a chair have that a stroller doesn't? The Lalo chair was the first minimalist high chair. The chair itself was a visual hammer; seeing the chair in a clutter-free living space communicated the modern aesthetic the brand was after.

It is important to start narrow, with one product and one enemy. The chair anchors the Lalo brand as the minimalist alternative to plastic furniture. Lalo has since expanded from the high chair to mealtime essentials like bibs and bento boxes. Recently they added playtime essentials like wooden play kitchens, table sets and play mats, and bathtime essentials like tubs, towels, and rinse cups. They can do this because they have a strong hero product in the mind: The Chair. The chair clearly represents how you can add your new baby to the family and still keep your home stylish.

The Young Men's Service League (The Enemy: Time)

Not all enemies are competing brands or categories. Sometimes the enemy is an idea, concept, or even time itself. The Young Men's Service League (YMSL) is a national organization that provides community service opportunities for moms and sons in high school. YMSL's four-year program requires moms to volunteer together with their sons for a minimum of 20 hours per year. What's the challenge? How to get moms to sign up during their son's eighth-grade year. It is a great program; I did it with both my sons. However, for busy mothers and their even busier sons, securing their commitment to the service hours, regardless of how worthwhile it is, can be challenging.

Identifying the strategic enemy was a key driver of the brand's positioning success. The enemy is the fast four years of high school. A mom with an eighth grader feels like she has been doing carpool, laundry, homework help, team mom duties, short-order cooking, and more forever. The reality is that in just four more years, her little boy will be 18 years old and likely to leave the nest by going to college, trade school, or work.

Yet at that moment during the winter months of middle school, it feels like high school graduation will never arrive. You have plenty of time with him, even too much you think. But you don't. I can tell you from personal experience that you get to that senior year in the blink of an eye. The nights are long, but the years go quickly. During the spring of your son's senior year, as moms we all reflect. The past four years, what have I instilled in my son, how much quality time did we spend together, what examples have I set, what will he remember? Will he grow up to love, respect, and give back to the world and his community?

Fear is a powerful motivator. Presenting moms with the enemy is effective. It illustrates how what feels like a chore in the short term will ultimately lead to satisfaction in the long run. How do you want to feel at graduation?

YMSL chapters have an annual banquet that all grades attend. The highlight is celebrating the journey of the senior moms and sons. Our chapter has each son record a video message to his mom thanking her and reflecting on the past four years of service together. The complied videos are played for all at the banquet.

Each video is practically the same and goes something like this. "Hi, Mom! Let's be honest, I wasn't thrilled you signed me up for this YMSL thing, but I am so glad you did. Spending time together volunteering was meaningful and memorable. I remember serving together at this philanthropy and that one. You set an example for service, compassion, and dedication that I will cherish and intend to continue."

There is rarely a dry eye in the house. The freshman moms are instantly reassured they made the right decision. They drag their sons with them to serve the community the next weekend.

Positioning (The First Enemy: Creative Advertising)

As I mentioned in the preface, the launch of positioning itself used a strategic enemy to build the idea. Reflecting on this made me even more excited to write this book.

Fifty years ago, when my dad and Jack Trout launched "positioning," the traditional way to build a brand was "creative" advertising. Bill Bernbach, the most famous advertising person at the time, said, "Properly practiced, creativity can make one ad do the work of ten."

My dad and Jack didn't just promote the benefits of the positioning theory. They purposely selected "creativity" as the strategic enemy when they launched it.

One of their typical positioning quotes at the time: *"Creativity is not the best way to build a brand in the mind. The best way to build a brand is by finding an open hole in the prospect's mind and then positioning the brand to fill that open hole."*

My father was incredibly proud of the lasting impact and legacy of his positioning theory. Positioning nailed the enemy and won. Today there is little doubt that positioning matters more than creativity in building a brand. When you open the brand building folder in the mind, positioning is the dominant brand.

Core Concepts: The Strategic Enemy

- When you define what you're against, it becomes clear what you are for.
- The mind understands opposition faster than superiority.
- The strategic enemy could be a competitor, category, concept or convention.
- The strategic enemy of a new category is the old category.

Chapter 4

Don't Be Your Own Worst Enemy

[Illustration of two Coca-Cola cans: "Coca-Cola CLASSIC" and "Coca-Cola *Life*"]

For many companies their own brand extensions stand in the way of finding an enemy. When a brand has line extended into every possible direction, they no longer have one position to stand on or enemy to fight against. Too often line extensions even make an enemy and fool of your own core brand. Don't forget line extensions say something about the original. Not to mention when one name is on everything it loses it meaning in the mind of the consumer.

■ ■ ■

While creativity was the original enemy of positioning, today the enemy is brand extension, which is taking the name of an established brand and using it on a new product or service. Logic is on the side of line extension working. Reality, unfortunately, is usually not.

What's wrong with line extending a brand? It is the result of the logical inside-out thinking that plagues most companies. Arguments for line extension include economics, trade acceptance, consumer acceptance, lower advertising costs, increased income, and corporate image. Why launch a new brand when we can use the well-known brand we already have?

The reason has nothing to do with logic, but everything to do with the mind. When your brand owns a position in the mind, the brand name is a surrogate for the product and category itself. When that name is on two or more categories, it messes with your mind.

First, the line extension dilutes the sharp focus of what your brand stands for. Second, it educates the consumer that your product isn't special; it is nothing more than a company name. Third, the line extension has no enemy, it leads to you becoming your own worst enemy.

Don't Fall in Love with Your Brand Name

When brands get big, they often get cocky. They fall in love with themselves and their names. Research shows that people's brains perk up when they hear their own name. I suspect company loyalists feel the same way when they hear their brand's name. Dale Carnegie famously said, "Remember that a person's name is to that person the sweetest and most important sound in any language." He recommended using it often in conversation to flatter and influence others.

When companies consider using their brand name on new product categories, it sounds great to them. They often attribute their success to the name itself, so putting that name on other stuff, any stuff, will make that stuff succeed too. Right?

Wrong. Names are not magic. Names are most powerful when they represent the category or a singular concept. Volvo is a brand name strongly associated with safety; they didn't have much luck trying to sell Volvo convertibles. Xerox is a name strongly associated with plain paper copiers; they didn't have much luck trying to sell Xerox computers. Coca-Cola is a name strongly associated with cola; they didn't have much luck trying to sell Coca-Cola energy drinks.

Consider a few more examples:

- What's a Chevrolet? A cheap, expensive car, truck, SVU, sports-car, gas, electric vehicle. It used to be the leader. Today, Chevrolet is just a name with no meaning. The leading car brand is Toyota. What's a Toyota? Reliable.
- What's a Scott? A toilet paper, paper towel, napkin, facial tissue. It used to be the leader. Now it is just a name. Scott invented toilet paper on a roll. Today, the leader in toilet paper is Charmin. What's a Charmin? Soft.
- What's a Yahoo? A search engine, newsfeed, email, messenger. While Yahoo was expanding to be a diversified web portal, Google focused. What's a Google? Search.

Instead of extending your brand name into multiple categories, using multiple brands is a better approach. Even if you need to buy them. The best thing Facebook did was buy Instagram. The best thing Google did was buy YouTube. The best thing Coca-Cola did was take a significant equity stake in Monster Energy.

Bayer Acetaminophen?

Aspirin was invented by the German company Bayer and patented in 1899. The drug was a game changer for reducing pain, inflammation, and fever. As a result, its popularity soared in the twentieth century and is still one of the most widely used medications in the world.

Interestingly, Aspirin was originally the brand name, but after World War I under the Treaty of Versailles, Bayer lost its trademark on "Aspirin" in most of the world. No matter—as the pioneer and original, Bayer retained its leadership and is still synonymous with aspirin and pain relief. The brand dominates the market and the mind. But like most categories, every drug will eventually face competition and enemies in the form of newer drugs.

In 1955, McNeil Laboratories launched its acetaminophen brand called Tylenol and positioned it against the enemy, aspirin. Tylenol touted that it provided similar pain relief but was easier on the stomach and would not increase the risk of bleeding.

The rising success of Tylenol did not go unnoticed at Bayer. So, what did they do?

Bayer introduced an acetaminophen product of its own and called it "Bayer Non-Aspirin Pain Reliever." It would be funny if it weren't true.

Typical inside-out thinking at work. At Bayer, they figured consumers that were buying Tylenol would now switch back to Bayer, the leading name in pain relief.

Not a chance. Bayer didn't own "pain relief" in the mind; it owned aspirin.

What ultimately worked out for Bayer was research that revealed the benefits of taking aspirin as a preventative measure against heart attacks and strokes. You see, the risk of bleeding from aspirin is due to its antiplatelet effect. Tylenol called that out as bad news, but it can be helpful for many hearts and minds. Aspirin helps to prevent blood clots from forming, which is a major cause of heart attacks and strokes. In 2022, earlier guidelines were reversed, now daily aspirin is no longer recommended for the primary prevention of cardiovascular disease.

Despite the failure of Bayer Non-Aspirin, Bayer refused to give up on its line-extension dreams. Too often companies blame execution instead of the line-extension strategy itself. In 1989, Bayer tried again and launched "Bayer Select," a line of various medications for headaches, menstrual pain, and cold symptoms. None of which contained any aspirin as an active ingredient. The results would give anybody a headache. They spent $110 million launching the brand, and the first-year sales totaled $25 million.

Coca-Cola Life?

Coca-Cola Life was born in 2014 to fill the great hole in the marketplace for a mid-calorie soda. This mythical hole is yet to be found, and the name is so bad that this case history is hard to believe. But it is all true.

How could one of the world's best companies launch a product with the name "Coca-Cola Life"? Seriously? It boggles the mind.

The name Coke "Life" instantly sets up the core product to be perceived as Coke "Death." Which isn't such a stretch in many people's minds; soda companies have been implicated as public enemy number one in the obesity epidemic.

In 2024, Mexico became one of the first countries to institute a soda tax. More are likely to follow. There is substantial evidence linking drinking soda to excessive calorie consumption and serious health risks that can lead to premature death. As a result, sugar is perceived by many as a killer.

Coca-Cola is clearly worried both on the consumer and PR fronts. However, more line extensions are unlikely to get them out of the hole; it is likely to just dig them in deeper. Adding more options isn't the answer. Too many choices led to confusion not clarity. If there is one quote that sums up the trap of line extension thinking, it is this:

"The power of choice is at the center of our strategy," said Oana Vlad, Coca-Cola brand manager. "Coke Life provides a great-tasting option for people looking for a Coke with alternative sweeteners."[1]

Coca-Cola already had Diet Coke, Diet Coke with Splenda, and Coca-Cola Zero. Lack of choice hardly seemed to be the issue. Consumers don't always want more choices; they want you to help guide them to feel good about making one clear choice.

Coca-Cola just could not let go of this idea that a huge untapped market lies between their regular and diet products. Even if this mythical mid-calorie soda category is feasible, it would be unlikely to succeed with a name like Coca-Cola Life.

Coca-Cola seems to also have a short memory. As George Santayana warned us, "Those who cannot remember the past are condemned to repeat it."

In 2004, Coca-Cola tried this same mid-calorie cola approach when they launched C2. Presumably the execution was wrong, not the strategy. C2 was heavily promoted as having all the great Coke taste with half the carbs and calories. Nobody was buying it. Most people pick one or the other depending on the moment. Great taste or no calories. As a result, C2 was a dismal flop and discontinued shortly after its big debut.

Life, of course, was going to be better. It was in a green can and had stevia leaf extract along with corn syrup or sugar. Green, I presume, to distinguish it from Coca-Cola in the red cans and signal how healthy it was.

Discontinued in 2020, Coca-Cola Life did not live very long. It was quickly forgotten by most.

The launch of line extensions is often done as a reaction to competition. Another category takes off or a new sweetener arrives, and the company tries to cover it with a line extension. Sounds logical but it rarely works. Consumers crave the real thing, not the imitation or copycat version. Being perceived as the real thing is why Coca-Cola is so powerful in the first place and why they are so hard to beat.

Coca-Cola Coffee?

Since the arrival of Starbucks, coffee has been hotter than ever. The trend did not go unnoticed at Cola-Cola. However, the reaction wasn't to launch a new coffee brand but to line extend its cola brand. The first attempt was back in 2006 with Coca-Cola Blak, a unique coffee-flavored cola. I remember trying it and still can't get the taste out of my mouth. It was done by 2008.

As with so many things, companies blame the execution and try again. Could improving the taste and adding real coffee make it work? In 2021, they did that and launched Coca-Cola with Coffee. It didn't taste as horrible as Blak, but it didn't make sense. Either you want coffee or cola. Mixing them together was weird. You should never mess with the real thing. Cola-Cola Coffee was gone by 2022. However, you can still find it in Canada; Canadians are too polite to tell the company how terrible it is.

Coca-Cola Energy?

Coca-Cola took one final stab in finding its own success in the energy drink category by line extending the real thing and launching Coca-Cola Energy in 2020. Coca-Cola Energy contained 114 mg of caffeine (three times the amount of a regular Coke) plus guarana extracts and B vitamins all with the familiar taste of Coke. The product was available in regular, cherry, and the no-sugar varieties to complement your upbeat and busy life according to the company.

The product filled a hole in the portfolio, not a hole in the mind. It was discontinued 16 months later. The press blamed clashing brand identities. Exactly. Don't put one name on two category folders in the mind.

Simply Too Much?

Simply Orange was launched in 2001 by Minute Maid (a division of Coca-Cola). The shifting trends were clear; Americans wanted more natural, additive-free foods. Minute Maid was losing the orange juice war with a line extension, so they launched a new brand to better fight the leader Tropicana. It worked great; then they simply went nuts with it.

Tropicana built its brand on flash pasteurization, which allowed them to be the first fresh chilled, not-from-concentrate orange juice. Its iconic straw-in-the-orange visual hammer communicated their advantage over the enemy: frozen concentrate. Tropicana was fresh from the orange, like sticking a straw in an orange and drinking straight from it.

Minute Maid was the pioneer in frozen concentrate, which accounted for the bulk of the market for decades. In the late 1960s, frozen accounted for 80 percent of juice sold.

By the late 1970s, Tropicana was making progress, and the fresh juice category accounted for 31 percent of juice sold. Minute Maid entered the fresh market with a line extension of its frozen concentrate brand. Backed by Coca-Cola's deep pockets, Minute Maid did have one initial advantage. It became the first national brand of chilled juice. Tropicana was a regional brand, with its main stronghold in New York City. In the twentieth century, several leading brands were built this way, including Budweiser, which was the first nationally available beer.

The Minute Maid chilled juice line extension was initially a winner. But time was not on their side. As the market shifted to fresh being dominant, the focused Tropicana brand that owned fresh from oranges positioning took over.

In 1990, Tropicana claimed category leadership with 22.3 percent overtaking Minute Maid with 22.2 percent. And they haven't looked back. By the year 2000, Tropicana dominated the market with 33 percent.

A Minute Maid line extension was never going to be able to effectively compete against Tropicana. What was needed was a new brand focused on not-from-concentrate with a new twist. That brand was Simply Orange.

Simply Orange is focused on natural ingredients and is sold in a distinctive clear contoured plastic bottle with a green twist cap. The clear bottle was different and unique. The enemy, Tropicana, was sold in paper cartons.

Simply has been a fierce competitor to Tropicana and is now a strong number two brand. Market shares as of May 2024 are as follows:

- Tropicana: 30.3 percent
- Simply: 26.6 percent
- Minute Maid: 3.6 percent

Simply's clear bottle is its visual hammer, which greatly enhances its visibility and appeal on shelves. While Tropicana switched to plastic in 2011 too, Simply was first.

In 2006, Simply expanded its presence in the fresh juice. This makes sense. One product in particular, Simply Lemonade, has been an especially big hit. It is the leading refrigerated lemonade. Simply selling a variety of juice flavors doesn't undermine the brand's core positioning of healthy juice in a plastic bottle.

However, the recent Simply line extensions are of greater concern. In 2022, Simply Spiked Lemonade was launched in collaboration with Molson Coors. Simply is a brand super popular with families and kids. Adding alcohol to the brand is dodgy. How many kids are going to grab one from the fridge thinking it is just Simply in a can?

The latest line extension to arrive is Simply Pop Prebiotic Soda, launched in February 2025. Why did they do this? Olipop and Poppi are gaining sales and attention. In 2024, Olipop had sales of $448 million and Poppi $370 million.

Coca-Cola just loves the line extension game, but it doesn't work or win. It didn't work for Coca-Cola, and it didn't work for Minute Maid. The brand that pioneers the category has all the advantages. To compete with it, you need to launch a new brand and position it as the opposite of the leader in some way. Simply was a success because it did just that. Don't they ever learn?

Coca-Cola needs to leave Simply alone. Its anchor is all-natural juice in a clear bottle. Simply was on track to potentially dethrone Tropicana one day. These line extensions are not helping the brand; they are watering down the juice.

In terms of prebiotic soda, perhaps Olipop and Poppi have discovered the holy grail of the mid-calorie soda. Olipop's Vintage Cola flavor has 35 calories. But it isn't positioned that way. It is a new kind of healthy soda that is high in fiber, with less sugar and prebiotics. It is sweetened with juice concentrates (sugar) and Stevia. It's a little like Coke Life with better branding.

Oatly Super Basic?

"Wow No Cow" is Oatly's battle cry. Oatly said no to cow milk and made milk for humans. The idea emanated from research at Lund University in Sweden in the 1990s, where scientists developed an enzymatic process that turned oats into a nutritious liquid that was formulated to be an alternative to dairy milk. This research laid the groundwork for Oatly, the original oat milk.

Coffee drinks were the first popular application for oat milk. Baristas and consumers alike appreciated oat milk's creamy texture and slight sweetness that complemented the coffee's bitterness. Oatly made its mark in cafes and among coffee enthusiasts.

In 2024, Oatly reported annual sales of $823 million. Sales are strong. But as a company gets bigger, huge annual growth numbers are harder to achieve. In 2000, Oatly's annual growth was 106 percent. In 2021, it was 52 percent. In 2024, it was only 5 percent. When growth slows, often the response is line extension: "We need more things to sell." While adding some new products might be called for, you need to be careful.

When the new line extension makes your original and best-selling product look bad, you become your own worst enemy. Oatly Super Basic is this type of line extension.

Honestly, I never looked at the ingredients in oat milk. I trusted Oatly oat milk to be healthy and clean. It is the leader and brand that built the category. I picked original, low-fat, or full fat. When they added Oatly Super Basic to their lineup, my choice became difficult.

The Super Basic line extension is basically saying to the world that the original has too many extra ingredients. So now I feel bad buying the original. It also instantly led me to do what many will do: check out the ingredients.

Original Oatly consists of the following: "Oat base (water, oats). Contains 2 percent or less of: low erucic acid rapeseed oil, dipotassium phosphate, calcium carbonate, tricalcium phosphate, sea salt, dicalcium phosphate, riboflavin, vitamin A acetate, vitamin D2, vitamin B12."

As soon as you read all that, you think, "Oh gosh, why do they have all this stuff in there? Rapeseed oil? Is that good or bad? Not sure. Dipotassium phosphate? Sounds scary. They use that in fertilizers but also imitation creamers."

Then you read the ingredients of Oatly Super Basic: Oat base (water, oats), sea salt, citrus fiber.

Super basic sounds super simple. And the choice is confounding. The extra ingredients such as oil and texturizers presumably are what makes it taste better, which then leads consumers to believe the basic won't taste good.

At this point, I think perhaps I will just go back to Fairlife. That brand is simple to understand. More protein, less sugar. They are probably very nice to the cows, and I am a lacto-vegetarian, not vegan.

Oatly had a choice. If being simple was better, why not just update all the Oatly products to be simple and clean?

The Oatly Super Basic line extension is like a billboard that says, "Hey, you, in case you didn't notice, our Oatly Original is full of added extras you may not want! Sorry we have fooled you for so long, but you can switch to our Oatly Super Basic that is actually healthy and wholesome."

Oatly Super Basic undermines the position of the original. The enemy of Super Basic is Oatly Original. How could it *not* be? Both fight each other, and Oatly ends up losing.

Budweiser: Line Extension Catches Up with the King

The damage caused by line extensions isn't always immediate. Meaning, some brands can get away with it for years and be successful. But no matter what, it will slowly weaken your anchor, and if a big storm comes, you might be left adrift with a brand that no longer stands for anything.

While your line extension might work now, there is always the next generation to think about. When they see your line extended brand, they can't remember your glorious past; they aren't sure what you stand for and only see your current mess. This is exactly what happened to Bud Light.

Light Beer: The First Enemy Was Regular Beer

Miller Lite was the pioneer in light beer, but even with its incredible "Tastes Great, Less Filling" idea with a line extension name, it was vulnerable. In a war between line extensions, guess who ultimately wins? The leader. Bud Light was introduced in 1982, seven years after Miller Lite expanded nationally.

Light beer wasn't a winner out of the gate. Regular beer was still king and far outsold light. In 1985, despite all the advertising from Miller Lite and Bud Light, light beer only accounted for about a third of the market.

At this point, the enemy of light beer was regular beer. That put Miller, Budweiser, and Coors in a bind. They needed to market their light line extensions without damaging their regular beer brand. Not easy. That is why launching a new brand of light beer without the "light" name would have been such a great move.

Budweiser, as the King of Beers, should have strongly taken a position against the enemy, light beer, and called it out as watered-down brew. But they couldn't. They kept silent on the enemy and stuck to the Clydesdales, frogs, and "Wassup" guys.

Bud Light should have strongly taken a position against the enemy, regular beer, as having way too many calories and carbs. Look how fat the King got by drinking that stuff. But they couldn't. So, they did Spuds and created a party boy image for the brand.

In 1987, Bud Light made its mark with a Super Bowl ad starring a bull terrier named Spuds MacKenzie—known as "Bud Light's original party animal!" Spuds became a pop-culture sensation and set the brand on a path to be most associated with fun-loving frat boys.

In 1994, Bud Light surpassed Miller Lite and trailed only Budweiser in sales. In 2001, Bud Light passed Budweiser to become America's best-selling beer, period. You would think Budweiser played it perfectly. The truth is they got lucky, and then sadly they got stupid drunk on line extension.

They were lucky because no light beer brand was ever launched that wasn't a line extension. So, the strength of Budweiser boosted Bud Light. And Bud Light was boosted by the light beer category becoming larger than the regular one.

Light Beer: New Enemies

At the turn of the twenty-first century, while light beer was dominant, other changes were brewing. Mexican food, drinks, and brands were on the rise. Mexican cuisine became the leading type of ethnic food restaurant. The margarita and the mojito became top cocktails. And Corona Extra, with its lime in the bottle, became the leading imported beer, overtaking long-time leader Heineken.

New categories were also emerging that particularly appealed to the younger generation, such as Mike's Hard Lemonade, launched in 1999, and Twisted Tea, launched in 2001. Later to come would be the killer wave, White Claw in 2016.

The early 2000s was a time Budweiser and Bud Light should have considered joining forces and uniting under one Budweiser brand identity as the King of Beers. The enemy was no longer other beer brands, light or otherwise, like it was in the 1980s and 1990s. The new enemy was twisted, hard, and Mexican.

Budweiser as a unified brand could focus on beer and being an American icon. An all-American classic in original and light. It is the strategy Coca-Cola is using now. Coca-Cola and Coca-Cola Zero Sugar are marketed as one brand in identical red packaging. The displays in stores are a sea of red. Coca-Cola is one brand against its enemies.

Budweiser and Bud Light are not united at all. Never have been. In fact, they used to hold an annual Bud Bowl during the Super Bowl where cartoons of brand bottles would play each other on the field to see who would win. The websites are separate. The advertising is separate. Budweiser is red. Bud Light is blue. That used to be how Coca-Cola and Coke Zero did it too. But Coke got wise, Budweiser didn't.

Bud Light's response to these new enemies was not to unite but to fire back with an endless barrage of line extensions. It worked once before, and they hoped it would work again. It hasn't. Bud Light started a slow decline that ended with it losing its leadership in America to Modelo Especial.

On April 1, 2023, things came to a head, when transgender influencer Dylan Mulvaney was hired to promote Bud Light. Using Mulvaney was only one part of a larger campaign intended to change the "fratty" image of Bud Light. Changing a widely held perception after four decades was unlikely to work. Instead, it sparked outrage and boycotts among its core and loyal base. Kid Rock filmed himself blasting cases of Bud Light with a rifle. Suddenly, Bud Light was enemy number one in the wokeness war.

The impact to the bottom line was swift. That year Bud Light lost $1.4 billion in sales, and the company lost over $27 billion in value.

But the issues at Bud Light were years in the making. The brand anchor had been greatly weakened by line extensions. The Mulvaney incident was a flash storm that accelerated the brand's demise.

What's a Bud Light?

To me the downfall of Bud Light began in 2008 with the launch of Bud Light Lime. A line extension meant to take on Corona. It was nonsense.

And the insanity continued from there with the launch of extensions like these:

- Bud Light Lime Lime-A-Rita, Staw-ber-Rita, Mang-o-Rita, Grape-a-Rita
- Bud Light Lemonade Lager, Orange Lager, Grapefruit Lager
- Bud Light Next: Zero Carbs
- Bud Light Platinum: 6%
- Bud Light Chelada
- Bud Light Seltzer: Classic flavors, Retro Tie Dye flavors
- Bud Light Hard Soda: Cola, Citrus, Orange, Cherry Cola
- Bud Light Platinum Seltzer: 8%

And they just keep coming.

Remember, consumers don't pick the brand and then decide which drink to have. They don't say, "I want a Bud Light product; should I have a Seltzer, Lima-A-Rita, or a Next?" Consumers decide the category first, then the brand. The brand that owns the category is in the best position to be selected.

- If you want a hard seltzer, you grab a White Claw.
- If you want a spirit seltzer, you grab a High Noon.
- If you want a light/athletic beer, you grab a Michelob Ultra.
- If you want an authentic Mexican beer, you grab a Modelo Especial.
- If you want the King of Beers, you grab a Budweiser.
- If you want a stout, you grab a Guinness.
- If you want a craft beer, you grab a Sam Adams.
- If you want a Belgian white, you grab a Blue Moon.
- If you want an alcohol-free beer, you grab an Athletic.

The list goes on, and in each case the brand that owns the category is the winner. And the less line extended, the better.

My sons are in their 20s, and younger consumers like them don't remember when Bud Light was just a beer and not a mess. To them it's a sellout. They have grown up seeing it on a ridiculous variety of products and line extensions.

And now they mostly remember the Mulvaney controversy and fallout.

New categories and new enemies pose a challenge. But line extension is rarely the answer. Maintaining focus is what keeps you strong. As a company, you should launch your own new brands in new categories or buy new brands launched by others.

It could have ended differently. Budweiser and the Clydesdales are like Coca-Cola and the contour bottle. A classic, iconic all-American visual hammer. Budweiser's can is iconic, distinctive, and powerful. Budweiser and Bud Light should have united into one Budweiser brand and then proclaimed themselves as the King of Beers and our American hero in original and light.

Being American isn't always perceived as a benefit, and it's not. It doesn't appeal to everybody. But when being American is your heritage and the best thing you have going for you, best not to go rogue and break all the positioning rules.

Keeping the Enemy in Mind

Sometimes your brand needs to evolve with the times. Other times your brand needs to refocus on its original mission. When it comes down to a decision on a line extension, ask yourself this: "Will this line-extension go against the focus of our brand and deprive us from having an enemy?"

Chipotle Puts Its Burrito in a Bowl

Chipotle, the king of burritos, launched its burrito bowl in the early 2000s for people looking to cut carbs and the tortilla from their burrito experience. Chipotle owns burritos in the mind. Does offering a burrito in a bowl undermine this position or not? I say it doesn't.

First, they wisely called it a burrito bowl, not a salad. This communicates that it is everything you want in your burrito but in a more convenient bowl. The bowl is also not round; it is in the same shape as the burrito itself, visually communicating the burrito positioning idea. The process for creating the bowl and the ingredients in it are the same as a burrito. Instead of wrapping the rice, beans, meat, lettuce, cheese, guacamole, salsa, and more in a tortilla, it just goes in a bowl.

Today, bowls are the most popular item at Chipotle and represent about two-thirds of orders. In the mind, Chipotle is still a burrito, but more easily eaten from a bowl. Evolution at work. The enemy is still burgers and chicken sandwiches that the other places serve.

The success of Chipotle's bowls has led many chains to add bowls to the menu. Suddenly bowls are everywhere. But they are not for every brand.

Smoothie King: The Launch of a New Category

Take Smoothie King. Founder Steve Kuhnau invented the smoothie category and gave it its name. Kuhnau grew up with extreme food allergies, especially to dairy, wheat, and nuts. It was a challenge to prepare meals to give his body nutrients, so one day as a teenager, he grabbed his mom's blender and dumped in fruits, vegetables, protein, and vitamins. He loved it and started making his blend all the time. Later, in his twenties, while working as a nurse in a burn unit, he thought his concoction might help his patients' wounds heal. They enjoyed his healthy and tasty drinks too.

Kuhnau was inspired, left his job, and opened The Original Smoothie Bar in 1973 in his native New Orleans. He called his healthy blends "smoothies" because of their smooth, blended texture. A smoothie was not a milkshake; it was a new category.

In 1989, the name was changed to Smoothie King, and they began to franchise. But as a franchise system, they lost their way. They ditched the real fruit and added sugar and ice cream to the smoothies to expand their customer base beyond just health-conscious consumers. As one critic wrote, they "offered up Big Macs you sucked through a straw."[2] By 2010, while Smoothie King had 500 profitable locations, leadership openly wondered what the brand stood for anymore. Had they become their own worst enemy?

That is the same year Wan Kim, a franchisee from South Korea, came to visit Kuhnau. His mission was to convince Smoothie King to refocus the brand on its original mission. Smoothies with one purpose: health.

Smoothie King: Refocusing on Healthy

Wan Kim was a Smoothie King fanatic. After drinking them almost daily as an undergraduate student in Boston, he became a master franchiser back in Korea, where he opened 120 stores in eight years. His amazing success and enthusiasm for the brand let him to boldly propose to Kuhnau not only that Smoothie King get back to healthy but that he buy him out in order to execute the plan. Kim's pitch was simple: "I really love your mission, and I strongly believe that I'm the one who can carry it through and make it bigger for you."[3] Kuhnau said he would think about it.

A year later Kuhnau called Kim and said, "You should do this because you really do believe in our mission. You believe in what we do."[4]

After Kim became Smoothie King's CEO, he made returning to "Smoothies with a Purpose" his mission. However, he needed to fix the smoothies first. The franchisees did not exactly appreciate this new guy from Korea saying he wanted to lower the calorie counts and clean up the smoothies, which could nosedive sales. They were not interested in focusing on "healthy" and said some awful things. Kim stayed firm. He told franchisees that Smoothie King would now use only whole fruit, organic vegetables, and remove sugar and unhealthy additives.

Initially the results were not good. Expenses rose, because real fruit is costly. And sales plummeted, because the new healthy drinks tasted different. For years they worked on refining every smoothie

Don't Be Your Own Worst Enemy

on the menu. They tinkered with the recipes and ingredients, and Kim's team taste-tested everything. By 2019, Kim not only made the menu healthier by overhauling 70 percent of it, but they perfected the flavor of each smoothie.

Sales started skyrocketing. Average revenue per store went from $300,000 to $600,000. The franchisees that were against the changes were now believers. Focusing on the brand's original positioning, healthy smoothies, doubled store sales. And Smoothie King itself more than doubled in size and now has more than 1,200 locations.

Smoothies Should Come with a Straw, Not a Spoon

Then came the bowls. In April 2023, Smoothie King launched smoothie bowls and spoons. The enemy of Smoothie King is a spoon. Smoothies are healthy and easy to drink anywhere. The spoon is the exact opposite of what they stand for. Listen, are smoothie bowls going to put them out of business? Unlikely. But the bowls are an unnecessary distraction to operations and dilute the core smoothie perception.

A better direction is to launch more healthy smoothies that come with their signature red straw—something they are doing too. In 2024, Smoothie King became the first quick-service chain to offer a GLP-1 menu for customers on drugs like Ozempic. The menu of high-protein, fiber-rich, and zero-added sugar smoothies was developed in partnership with registered dietician Molly Kimball. The Ozempic crazy should be a boon to the smoothie business.

Line extensions seem to find their way into every company's playbook eventually. It takes diligence to remain focused. Maybe it was your predecessors who launched the line extensions. Don't be afraid to get rid of them. The best thing to do is occasionally take stock, refocus if needed, and courageously cut what is diluting your brand to ensure you don't become your own worst enemy.

> **Core Concepts: Don't Be Your Own Worst Enemy**
> - Don't fall in love and be blinded by your brand name.
> - Brands benefit from focus and are weakened by line extension.
> - Brand extensions often turn you into your own worst enemy.
> - Don't extend your brand into a new category, launch a new brand instead.

Chapter 5

The Power of Saying No

No is a powerful word. It's a hard line that instantly makes your position and the enemy clear. If you say yes to everything and everybody, there is little chance of finding a strategic enemy. More brands need to say no. Too few do. Instead, they run around constantly looking for what to say yes to next. Too many yeses are often what gets brands into trouble.

■ ■ ■

When it comes to perceptions, the customer is always right. What people perceive in their mind is reality regardless of the facts. The essence of positioning thinking is to accept these perceptions and then structure your message accordingly, so it is easily accepted by the consumer.

While the consumer's perceptions might be right, they can't always be trusted to know what is best for your brand. Many falsely take the adage of "the customer is always right" to mean "the customer should get whatever they ask for." This isn't necessarily a good motto to live by.

Knowing when to say no is critical. And it takes courage to do it. Saying no sends a strong message about what you stand for and what you are fighting against. It makes it instantly clear who your enemy is.

Chick-fil-A Said No to Burgers

In 1967, S. Truett Cathy founded and opened the first Chick-fil-A restaurant in Atlanta's Greenbriar Mall. Chick-fil-A is a near-perfect example of being first, saying no, and maintaining focus and consistency for decades.

It was Cathy's bold idea to launch his fast-food restaurant in a mall, and he was the first to do it. The food court as we know it today did not exist. Eating in the mall wasn't a thing. There were only a few options such as snack bars and candy shops. McDonald's and Burger King were on the rise but were stand-alone restaurants near the mall and not in the mall itself.

But it wasn't just being in the mall. Chick-fil-A was the first brand to focus on the fried chicken sandwich. After testing hundreds of recipes, Cathy perfected the Original Chick-fil-A chicken sandwich recipe with two pickles on a toasted butter bun. They have used the same recipe ever since, or so says the website.

Next came some critical nos. The first no was to be closed on Sundays. Not so unusual in the 1960s—many states still had blue laws requiring stores to be closed on Sundays to enforce religious standards such as observing a day of rest. But in the 1970s these laws were being greatly relaxed and spending Sunday at the mall was becoming a popular pastime.

However, Chick-fil-A has stuck by the practice of being closed on Sundays to give their employees the day off. As a fast-food giant, saying no to customers on Sunday seems foolish, but sticking with it has become a hallmark of the brand's values and lore. They celebrate it. Sometimes when you know you can't have something, somehow you crave it more. We had better go twice on Saturday!

Without a doubt, the most important decision of Chick-fil-A was to say no to selling hamburgers. The enemy of Chick-fil-A's chicken sandwich is the hamburger sandwich. Chick-fil-A is focused on chicken and has been riding the chicken category boom. Chicken, even fried chicken, has a healthier halo compared to beef and people are eating more of it. The US per capita consumption of chicken has risen from 33 pounds in 1960 to almost 100 pounds today. Your success is greatly dependent on the category.

In 1995, Chick-fil-A began dramatizing their beefy enemy with their iconic cows who constantly are reminding us to "Eat Mor Chikin." The campaign greatly increased the brand's visibility. However, I can only imagine the pitch meeting when the ad agency boldly presented that the campaign would feature cows telling people not to eat them. What?! A crazy company might run the campaign for 6 months; Chick-fil-A as a smart company has stuck with their cows for 30 years.

Thanks to its focus on chicken, operation excellence, and marketing prowess, Chick-fil-A is now the third-largest restaurant chain in the United States by sales. It's growth has been tremendous. Chick-fil-A's has doubled its total sales volume since 2018.

In 2023, Chick-fil-A's annual sales were $21.6 billion with 2,552 locations, behind McDonald's with $53 billion in sales and 13,457 locations and Starbucks with $28.7 billion in sales and 16,346 locations.[1]

Rounding out the top 12 chains are Taco Bell, Wendy's, Dunkin', Burger King, Subway, Chipotle, Domino's, Panera Bread, and Panda Express. Notice the trend? Being different and focused as a brand is what gets you to the top.

"Eat Mor Chikin" is the poster child for having an enemy. It all started with the courage to say no. After that, you need to dramatize and visualize your difference then repeat it for decades.

The Power of Saying No

Southwest Airlines Said No to First Class

Most brands try to appeal to everyone and rarely say no. Airlines are a key example. Almost all offer first class, business class, economy plus, regular, basic, and more. Airlines pride themselves on the pricing optimization of every seat, proudly telling investors how they are squeezing the most money out of each customer. This makes sense in the market, but not in the mind.

Having more choices doesn't necessarily lead to more satisfaction. It is stressful buying a ticket on most airlines. Too many choices and too many price points make figuring out the best deal difficult. Then when you get to the plane, they rub that choice in your face. Sit in first class and feel stupid for how much money you paid, or march past the big comfy seats to the back of the plane and feel cheap. Most airline brands are not loved but tolerated, except for Southwest.

Southwest did the opposite. Founder Herb Kelleher pioneered the low-cost airline category by focusing on short-haul flights, high-frequency departures, and minimal service differences among passengers. Among the nos were: no first class, no seat assignments, no food, no pets, no inter-airline baggage transfers. These nos allowed Southwest to cut its cost and offer consumers super-low fares, which helped make air travel more accessible and affordable to a broader audience.

Southwest focused operations too and exclusively operated one type of aircraft, the Boeing 737. Having a single-type fleet greatly simplified operations, including maintenance, training, and scheduling. This kept efficiency high and costs low. Southwest has one of the strongest safety records in aviation; when you fly only one type of aircraft training, maintenance and safety are maximized.

The experience of flying Southwest was dramatically different; it was a one-class airline where everybody was equal. No curtain pulled after take-off to separate the first-class from the second-class fliers. That silly curtain. Is it supposed to protect the rich people in the front from the rest of us in the back of the plane?

While Southwest did not serve meals, they did famously hand out peanuts. Peanuts were a great metaphor for the brand. We would have dramatized it by using the slogan "Fly for Peanuts." However, in 2018 Southwest decided to say no even to its much-loved peanuts. Why? Peanut allergies.

When I fly Delta, occasionally the flight attendant will get on the speaker to make an announcement: "So sorry to inform you, but we are unable to serve nuts on this flight due to a passenger with a nut allergy." People like me who love nuts on board usually groan, sigh, and covertly look around with piercing eyes to see which passenger is the cause of the nut-less flight. Unsympathetic yes, but human.

Southwest made the tough choice to remove all nuts to streamline operations and make all travelers welcome. Another no for the sake of making the passenger experience and to treat all consumers alike. (Honestly, it must feel terrible to be the person with a nut allergy when they make the announcement on Delta. Nobody likes being called out publicly for something they have no control over.)

Currently Southwest is under pressure from activist investors to boost revenues by following in the footsteps of the major carriers. In 2025, they plan to add seat selection, premium seating, baggage fees and more, all of which will slowly undo what made Southwest special.

Brands do need to evolve and make necessary changes. Like when Southwest removed nuts. The chaos and stress of boarding with no assigned seating was becoming problematic. Many people tried to game the boarding system and cheated by saving seats for others. It certainly was getting difficult to manage and less enjoyable for passengers. Adding assigned seating for the sake of the passenger experience is a wise move. It could have been done in a Southwest way that was inclusive and fair. But premium seating? This goes against the essence of the brand itself. Herb Kelleher must be rolling over in his grave. Premium seating will weaken the brand in the long term. My guess is Southwest has a hard time saying no to investors that are seeking short-term profits over long-term branding.

With all these changes, Southwest is at risk of losing its low-cost brand anchor. The final straw came in March 2025 when Southwest announced that bags will no longer fly free. Seat assignments will benefit customers; bags not flying free is an outrage.

The Power of Saying No

In July 2024, CEO Bob Jordan, when speaking to analysts, reconfirmed the importance of this signature perk. "Just to be real clear on bags fly free as a policy, I mean, we're not looking at this point to change that policy," he said, adding that "after fare and schedule, bags fly free is cited as the number-one issue in terms of why customers choose Southwest."[2]

Southwest should have hung on to this one last bastion that made the brand different. "Bags fly free" could have been the rallying cry of the company. It could have provided one specific, memorable, visual, and important reason to fly the airline. Without it they are no different than all the others.

In a video explaining why they are dropping the bags-fly-free policy, Jordan defended the decision this way: "It's about adapting to what our customers want. Our DNA isn't open seating or even bags fly free. It's a dedication to service and hospitality."[3]

He is wrong. The DNA of the company was open seating and bags flying free. Dropping the seating was one thing; dropping both is a disaster. Saying that customers want to pay for bags is also an insult. What customer wants to pay for bags? Or wants only A-List Preferred fliers to get the perk? The effect of charging for bags will only result in a dramatic increase in carry-on bags, which will lead to slower boarding times, overstuffed bins, and a diminished customer experience.

Southwest needs to maintain its low-cost, all-for-one mentality and focus. Simplicity, transparency, and bags flying free are essential elements of the brand if they want to continue to stand for something and have an enemy to rally against.

Salesforce Said No to Software

In 1999, Salesforce started from humble beginnings in a one-room apartment next to founder Marc Benioff's house atop Telegraph Hill in San Francisco. With posters of the Dalai Lama and Albert Einstein hanging on the wall, Marc and three friends began to build a new way to deliver business software applications. Their vision was to be an Internet company for salesforce automation. They built a CRM (customer relations management) application via a simple website instead of server-based software.

Using the Internet eliminated the multimillion-dollar up-front costs, implementations that can take years, and the ongoing complexities of maintenance and upgrades typical of installed software solutions. It was a trailblazing endeavor.

Salesforce is the pioneer of what we now call software as a service (SaaS). But radical change coming from a small company in an industry dominated by giants would not come easily. What Salesforce had to offer was amazing, but even the greatest ideas require time to build and bold marketing to get into the mind.

By 2000, Salesforce was armed with a great product, a great team, and a new office at One Market Street. Instead of focusing on the benefits of SaaS, Salesforce's first move was to call out and take down its enemy: software.

Salesforce officially launched with an event held at San Francisco's Regency Theater with 1,500 attendees. The mission from day one was to disrupt the status quo. Salesforce turned the lower level of the theater into an area that symbolized enterprise software and that they called "Hell." There were screaming "salespeople" actors in cages and games such as whack-a-mole where you could whack the names of other big software companies. Once attendees made their way through hell, they ascended to Salesforce.com. Pretty audacious stuff.

The next month, Salesforce was featured in the *Wall Street Journal* after hiring actors to stage a mock protest outside a Siebel Systems conference. The "protestors" carried signs with anti-software messages to drive home Salesforce's "The End of Software" battle cry. The visual hammer was the word software with a red "no" symbol across it.

The advertising for "The End of Software" featured a fighter jet shooting down a biplane. The fighter jet represented Salesforce, a technologically advanced, disruptive, and revolutionary company taking out what came before it. The biplane represented the software industry, obsolete and ill-suited for the mission.

In 2002, Benioff made a prediction about the future of Salesforce CRM: "There were the leaders, but Oracle displaced them. The same thing is going to happen again. It's the beginning of a brand new technology and business world."[4]

He was right. Salesforce displaced them all and is now the global leader in CRM with annual sales in 2024 of $34.9 billion and average revenue growth over the past ten years of 24 percent. Salesforce has united a global trailblazer community that celebrates using Salesforce to drive transformational change.

For years, Salesforce was focused on one message and visual: no software. After killing software, Salesforce now uses it logo with the blue cloud as a powerful visual hammer that communicates leadership.

In 2019, Benioff wrote a book entitled *Trailblazer* that gives a behind-the-scenes look at the inner working of Salesforce and credits its core values of trust, customer success, innovation, and equality as its greatest competitive advantage. Salesforce is the dominant leader of a revolutionary new category they created. Their greatest competitive advantage is leadership.

That said, it is noteworthy and admirable to see how they have built the company and developed its core values. Salesforce is regularly ranked as one of the best places to work and best workplaces for giving back. Dominance in the category has enabled them to not just do well but to also do good.

As of 2023, Salesforces has given more than $704 million in grants, 8.7 million hours of community service, and provided product donations for more than 56,000 nonprofits and educational institutions. A worthy example to follow but it's not what built the brand. Saying no to software did that.

Subaru Said No to Two-Wheel Drive

Subaru is the pioneer of all-wheel drive vehicles, a powerful focus that took the company more than 20 years to realize and leverage. Subaru pioneered all-wheel drive technology back in 1972, but they figured not all consumers wanted it or needed it, which is technically true. In the United States while all-wheel drive is particularly good in the snow and ice in the northern states, it's not really necessary in the southern ones.

Subaru's sales figures matched this assumption with half of its sales coming from two-wheel drive (52 percent) and the rest all-wheel drive (48 percent). The problem? The Subaru brand was in deep trouble and the company was losing a ton of money. In 1993, the brand was in 23rd place in the US market with sales of $1.4 billion dollars and losses of $250 million on these sales.

That year they fired the CEO and replaced him with George Muller. Muller led a strategic repositioning of Subaru that many in the industry cite as the most profound turnaround ever in auto history. Muller's solution to Subaru's problem was simple yet totally insane. Muller said no to making two-wheel drive cars, effectively reducing sales by 50 percent. Marketing isn't logical.

When Subaru was selling both two-wheel and all-wheel drive cars, it didn't have a focus, a clear message, or an enemy. As a result, it was a weak brand. It didn't take a lot of investment to turn around Subaru either; it just took a whole lot of courage.

In the year 2000, on the eve of his retirement, Muller summed up his success. "Look at what Subaru, a small auto company, has done. We differentiated ourselves around our strengths. We invented a category. We resurrected our brand ... all with a minimum of resources."[5]

Saying no is only step one. After Subaru said no to two-wheel drive, they focused on expanding and promoting all-wheel drive. They launched the Outback and Forester models that established the crossover all-wheel drive SVU category. They also promoted Subaru to a narrow target market. Subaru was for adventure-seeking outdoor enthusiasts. The snowy northern states were the initial focus, then in 2010 they expanded on that success to more aggressively promote the brand and its all-wheel drive in the south. The brand doesn't try to appeal to everyone; it is for people who love nature and lead active lifestyles. It turns out a lot of us aspire to Subaru's all-wheel drive positioning and what it stands for: practicality and performance.

Subaru for years has been one of the fastest-growing brands in the industry. In 1993, before they focused, they sold 104,179 vehicles. In 2024, Subaru sold 667,725 vehicles, which was a 5.6 percent increase from the year before and capped its twenty-ninth consecutive month of year-over-year sales gains. When you say no, you just might sell more.

Uniqlo Said No to Trends

Zara is the pioneer of fast fashion. The company revolutionized the fashion industry via its rapid-turnaround approach. Zara said no to placing big production orders in low-cost regions with long lead times. Instead, its tight vertical integration and near-shore production in places such as Spain, Portugal, and Morocco allow Zara to quickly respond to fashion trends. This helps keep inventory down, reducing the risk of unsold items. For the consumer, the advantage of shopping at Zara is that they always have the latest fashion trends in stock at affordable prices.

For most positions, there is an inverse position that can be equally as strong. Uniqlo's strategy is the exact opposite of Zara's. The brand's philosophy is to totally ignore fashion trends and focus on clothes items that are universal and timeless.

In 1972, Tadashi Yanai inherited his father's chain of 22 men's suit stores in Yamaguchi, Japan. Inspired by his travels abroad and seeing brands such as the Gap and Benetton, Yanai saw immense potential for a Japanese casual wear brand. After becoming president in 1984, he opened a new store in Hiroshima called the Unique Clothing Warehouse and shifted the company's focus from suiting to casual clothing. He followed the vertical integration strategy of other fashion brands such as Zara and H&M. Later the generic store name was shortened to Uniqlo.

By the early 2000s, Uniqlo had several hundred stores across Japan. But it also had a problem. It was perceived to be a discount retailer selling cheap and low-quality apparel. This perception was true. So Uniqlo did something to drastically change it. When a brand is small, drastic change is possible. When you have thousands of stores around the world, changing your perception in the mind is nearly impossible.

In 2004, Uniqlo introduced its Global Quality Declaration and pledged to stop making low-priced, low-quality garments. The first product to garner attention was its high-quality fleece jacket, this began the brand's shift from being perceived as cheap and low-quality in the mind to being affordable and high-quality.

Zara's brand was built on rapidly responding to fashion trends, getting items from factory to store in approximately two weeks.

Uniqlo takes the exact opposite approach, planning production of its wardrobe essentials up to a year in advance.

Unlike Zara, which sells a large variety of styles inspired by the global runway, Uniqlo focuses on producing a few styles of practical urban basics. They produce only two seasonal collections a year and half of the items are carried over from the previous season.

Tadashi Yanai is fond of saying, "Uniqlo is not a fashion company, it's a technology company."[6] Uniqlo's approach does indeed have much more in common with computing's iterative process where each successive iteration is built upon the previous one. This method allows for continuous assessment, enhancements, and successive versions which improve upon the last.

The company's ethos is about perfecting each piece. Uniqlo's lightweight down jacket is a great example. "It was launched 20 years ago, but it still sells in the millions because it's a timeless piece," according to Clare Waight Keller, Uniqlo's creative director. "Each season they make these little tweaks to improve it. Uniqlo has this saying: even if it's 99 percent perfect, it's still not perfect enough."[7]

Uniqlo dominates Japan where one in four people are said to own a Uniqlo jacket. It's the biggest apparel chain in Asia and is well on its way to becoming a global powerhouse. There are roughly 800 stores in Japan and 2,400 globally. With $22 billion in annual sales, it is currently in third place in the global rankings of fashion retailers, just behind Zara with sales of $33.7 billion and Sweden's H&M with sales of $24.3 billion. With only 60 stores in the United States, Uniqlo hasn't yet made its mark in America yet, but it is already bigger than Gap Inc. (sales $15.2 billion). The Gap should be worried; Uniqlo has an aggressive strategy planned with a target of 200 stores in North America by 2027.

Energy Bar Brands that Said No

PowerBar is the original energy bar. Founded in 1986 by a Canadian long-distance runner, it was the first bar designed to provide quick energy to enhance performance during prolonged exercise. As most candy bars, PowerBar was mainly sugar. Nothing is wrong with that;

when you are running a marathon, you need sugar. They took a bar of sugar and gave it a new category name: energy bar. Say no to candy and yes to PowerBar.

The success of PowerBar led to an explosion of energy bar brands. You don't win by being better; you do it by focusing and attacking your enemy where they are weak.

PowerBar is loaded with sugar and low in protein. In 2010, Quest Bars attacked by narrowing the focus to high protein and saying no to carbs. Quest Bars were not for endurance athletes but for regular people looking for a bar that was low in carbs and high in protein. While a Quest Bar contains 20–25 grams of total carbohydrates, the net carbs are much lower due to its high fiber content and the use of sugar alcohol. As a result, Quest Bars became popular for consumers on low-carb or ketogenic diets.

For every strong position, there is usually an alternative that is also viable. High-carb versus low-carb bars, for example. The energy bar category has given birth to many new categories. Success is driven by narrowing your focus, which is best done by finding something to say no to.

In 2013, RXBAR called bull on the ingredients found in other energy bar brands. RXBAR is the first No B.S. (No Bad Stuff) protein bar made with simple ingredients. RXBARs are committed to using no artificial colors, flavors, preservatives, or fillers.

While other bars might be high in protein, they are also loaded with ingredients no one can pronounce, a direct dig at its enemy Quest.

Many brands make claims, but few find powerful ways to visualize them. All food packages list the ingredients in small print on the back as required by law. RXBAR presents its ingredients as the key visual on the front of the package. Bold move.

RXBAR also explain their ingredients in specific and simple terms: three egg whites, two dates, six almonds. It is brilliant, different, and very effective. And while RXBAR isn't low in sugar like Quest, they anchor their brand with only using natural ingredients.

If you keep looking, there is always a way to say no to something and do things differently. What do PowerBar, Quest, and RXBAR have in common? They are all extruded. Extrusion is a manufacturing process where ingredients are mixed up together and then forced through an extruder into one long piece that is cut then packaged. This ensures each bite has a consistent texture and distribution of ingredients. It tastes great but doesn't look very pretty or natural.

KIND Bar said no to extrusion and was the first whole food energy bar. The enemy were all the extruded bars. KIND found a way to show this difference by using transparent packaging to showcase the whole ingredients such as nuts and chocolate drizzle. Seeing is believing. In 2025, KIND is working to replace their iconic clear packaging with paper wrappers. The see-through plastic was essential at the start, now switching to a more plant friendly package with a photo of the ingredients will work just as well.

GEM Said No to Pills

GEM is the first real-food multivitamin bite. GEM Health founder Sara Cullen, struggled for years with extreme fatigue, inflammation, and digestion issues. She discovered that like 90 percent of Americans, she was nutrient deficient despite eating "a perfect diet." But when she headed to the supplement aisle, she was met with pills and gummy chews filled with synthetic ingredients and artificial stuff. Driven by her passion for natural health solutions, Sara sought to create the first real-food multivitamin.

GEM provides a daily bite of essential nutrition you eat instead of swallowing pills. They originally tried to position GEM as strategic supplementation, something that isn't easily understood in the mind. Nor can it be visualized. Who is the enemy? Non-strategic supplementation?

Brands don't always get the messaging right at the start. They try to communicate too many ideas, don't keep it simple and fail to leverage the strategic enemy.

GEM recently revamped their website and now have called out their strategic enemy as synthetic supplement pills and found their focus. They promote "Gem vs. Them." GEM is Real Food Nutrients Bite vs. Synthetic Supplement Pills.

The purest source of vitamins comes from real food. GEM daily bites are a functional multivitamin formulated for proper

The Power of Saying No

absorption packed with 20+ vitamins, minerals, prebiotics, probiotics, and superfoods—all in one delicious real-food bite for foundational health.

Say Yes to Focus and No to Expansion

There are many telehealth companies that sell erectile solutions online. BlueChew does it only in chewable form. Is chewing better than swallowing a pill? Who knows. It certainly is more convenient and may work faster than pills. The chewable focus is a differentiator in a category filled with competitors that sell everything. It also isn't just a company name but the product itself. You do a BlueChew and buy it from BlueChew.com, which has greatly enhanced and accelerated its word of mouth.

The chewable focus led to a memorable slogan: "Chew it and Do it." They even sell a full line of BlueChew swag from hats to shirts, tank tops, and joggers. Can't say that about any other ED brands. Making the brand easy to talk about helps to reduce the stigma and makes it cool to use. So cool, people will wear swag.

Roman Health Ventures started with a focus on erectile dysfunction with its first product Roman. "Be Roman Ready" was the slogan, which was effective and memorable. Sadly, the success went to their head, and they expanded their offerings to include other health issues for both men and women, from weight loss to hair loss to fertility and menopause. Then shortened the name to Ro to serve as an umbrella brand for everything. Roman was better than Ro. Focusing on men was better than being for everybody.

Too many yeses gets companies in trouble. When you say no, your focus and the enemy is clear.

> **Core Concepts: The Power of Saying No**
> - Saying no takes courage.
> - Saying no is the easiest way to find your enemy.
> - Saying no is believable to the consumer.
> - Saying no keeps the company focused.

Chapter 6

When You Focus, the Enemy Is Clear

There are too many messages, brands, and concepts in the world. The only way to get noticed is to focus on one simple idea. To stand out from the crowd you start by standing for something specific. A focus is what builds a brand position in the mind. When you have a focus, the enemy will be clear. You will find your meaning and what your brand is fighting for.

■ ■ ■

The concept of focus is a key element of the positioning theory. A focus must be simple, memorable, different, and have an enemy. When you focus, you increase the power and ability for your brand to enter the mind of prospects.

The truth is every successful company usually starts out highly focused on an individual product, service, or market. But over time a company tends to become less focused by offering too many different products and services for too many markets at too many price levels. It often loses its sense of direction and what it stands for, forgetting where it is going and who the enemy is.

If you are an entrepreneur, you must focus, or you will not build a brand. Focusing at the early stages of the company comes naturally to most.

Once you are successful, things get more challenging. If the product turns out to be a winner, the company has momentum, and the stock price soars. Excitement and optimism fuel the urge to expand and branch out in all different directions. It also leads to arrogance that you can do no wrong and nobody can take you down.

If you allow the company to become too unfocused, after a while things will start going wrong. What seemed like endless opportunities can turn into endless problems. Objectives unmet. Sales flattening. Profits declining. The press unflattering. It happened to General Motors in the sixties. Sears in the seventies. IBM in the eighties. Sony in the nineties and Intel in the 2000s.

Maintaining a focus goes against nature. In science, it is known as *entropy*. The second law of thermodynamics states that the total entropy of any closed system will never decrease over time. Entropy is a measure of disorder in a system, and it tends to increase naturally. In marketing terms, it means that companies tend to become less organized and more dispersed unless a strong leader is there to maintain order and focus.

The constant pressure to grow the top line is what leads many companies to become unfocused, which is why a strong leader is so critical in navigating the company ship. Decisions on focus must come from the top. What to say no to. How to allocate resources. And what to focus on for the future.

A focus is not always forever. Even a powerful focus can become obsolete. Digital Equipment in minicomputers. Kodak in photography. iPod in hard-drive music players. But a focus is not a fashion statement either that needs to be changed every few years. A focus is more likely counted in decades, not years. Then, too, it depends on the category. The tech industry, for example, changes much faster than the toothpaste one. Colgate is 219 years old.

Sometimes a company may pivot its focus to capitalize on a new category or opportunity. Sticking to one focus at a time is what makes a company and brand genuinely great.

Halo Top: Calories in the Pint

In 2011, Justin Woolverton was a litigation lawyer working in Los Angeles and not looking to start a business. He was just a guy with a sweet tooth and a problem. Like a lot of us, he wanted to eat an entire pint of ice cream and not hate himself.

Justin craved something that tasted like ice cream but was healthier and low in calories and sugar. So, he bought a $20 ice cream maker on Amazon and started experimenting in his kitchen with ingredients including Greek yogurt, skim milk, eggs, sugar, and Stevia to perfect a delicious and guilt-free dessert. It was so good he thought, "If I like it, maybe a lot of other people will like it. We should bring it to market."[1]

By 2013, Woolverton had quit his job to work on his new product full-time. He also brought in a partner, Doug Bouton, a friend and former lawyer who recently quit his job to help him. The two lawyers, with no experience launching an ice cream company, were loaded with student loan debt and maxed-out credit cards. Not exactly the recipe for massive success.

Justin came up with the name Halo Top. It was brilliant, alluding to the category in a catchy and memorable way. Remember, his focus was on eating the whole pint. The halo over the pint of ice cream suggested the goodness and lightness of this new better-for-you brand.

There were other low-calorie products on the market such as Arctic Zero. But they used water instead of milk as the base, so unlike

Halo Top they didn't taste like ice cream. The light versions of traditional ice cream brands contained a ton of sugar and corn syrup, so consumers didn't see these as healthy alternatives. Halo Top's product was different and first of its kind.

Despite creating a unique product and using a great brand name, success did not come right away. Being different isn't enough. To stand out and be considered, you need to communicate your message quickly and clearly.

In 2015, with sales of around $1.4 million, the company made a critical change. The packaging was completely redesigned to be as distinct as the product itself and leveraged to hammer Halo Top's value proposition.

The original packaging mimicked every other brand on the shelf. The Halo Top Creamery name was the focal point. Below it promoted the serving size details including: 7 grams protein, 70 calories, and 4 net carbs. The overall impression was lackluster. Consumers need one reason to buy the product, not 10.

The enemy was the absurd serving size suggestions. Haagen Dazs' Vanilla Bean ice cream promotes having only 250 calories—sure, if you eat only one spoonful. The whole pint is 910 calories. A pint of Ben & Jerry's Gimme S'more! will set you back 1,250 calories and 72 grams of fat and 106 grams of sugar.

The new hero of the Halo Top package became the total calories of eating the whole pint. The vanilla bean pint showcased "280" in huge font with the name Halo Top in smaller type bending over it. It was a radically different approach than any other brand.

Luck often plays a role in success. But as the Roman philosopher Seneca said, "Luck is what happens when preparation meets opportunity." Halo Top's new package design along with its unique product set them up for opportunity to strike.

That is exactly what happened to Halo Top when *GQ* magazine ran a story in January 2016 titled: "What It's Like to Eat Nothing but This Magical, Healthy Ice Cream for 10 Days: Halo Top is low in calories, low in carbs, and loaded with protein. But is it too good to be true?" The article was too good to be true, and it lit the brand on fire. Soon Khloe Kardashian was snapping about it, top model Karlie

Kloss posted she was obsessed with it, and Instagram blew up with photos and posts raving about it.

The result was nothing less than extraordinary. By August 2017 Halo Top was the top-selling pint of ice cream in the United States, and *Time* Magazine named it one of the top inventions of the year. Sales skyrocketed to $347 million.

Wells Enterprises, the maker of Blue Bunny ice cream, acquired Halo Top in 2019. And guess what they did? Expanded the brand, of course. There are now Halo Top pops, fruit bars and even baking mixes. Box of Halo Top fudge brownie mix, anybody?

As you might expect, sales have fallen. Line-extension weakens a brand; it doesn't make it stronger. Big companies just can't help themselves it seems. They see line-extension as the only option to expand sales.

What should Wells have done with the brand? Keep it as focused as possible. The focus should be on continual improvement of the Halo Top main product and pricing. It's the real thing, but only if it comes in a pint and is low in calories.

Nike Loses Focus and New Brands Jump In

When the category leader loses focus, it spells opportunity. Nike has been the dominant leader for decades with its focus on performance athletic shoes. Nike's "Just do it" has for years brought inspiration and motivation to every athlete in the world. Nike's long roster of top athletes such as Michael Jordan, Serena Williams, LeBron James, and Cristiano Ronaldo represent the biggest winners in sports. Nike was used to winning. What happened recently shocked them, but it didn't shock me. When you lose focus on the key essence of your brand, the brand suffers.

"The Man Who Made Nike Uncool" read the September 2024 headline of a *Businessweek* story blaming then-CEO John Donahoe for driving down sales, pissing off partners, and disappointing fans. He was fired shortly after the article ran, and Nike was turned over to Elliot Hill, a Nike lifer who started as an intern.

What did Donahoe do? To sum it up Donahoe explained it this way when addressing investors: "The consumer told us they wanted a lifestyle product, and we delivered" after the company posted a record sales of $50 billion the year before.[2]

He should have read chapter 5 and just said no. In the short term, expanding from performance to fashion increased sales. But in the long term, this loss of focus weakens the brand.

In 2021, Nike released one of its most successful sneakers of all time, the Panda Dunk. It was a black-and-white revival of the low-top basketball shoe from the 1980s and was an instant hit. To meet demand, Nike started pumping out endless new Panda varieties and line extensions. The Pandas were a fashion and lifestyle play. Nike went way overboard on Pandas, it was one of many examples of Nike being distracted by fashion trends over sports and athletes.

Donahoe's strategy also focused on direct selling, cutting out the middlemen to increase margins. Retail has long been critical for sneakers, and there are a lot of retailers out there. Nike abandoned them and disappeared from the shelves. Leaders need visibility. Nike's history of dominating retail and sudden departure left a lot of open shelf space for other brands to fill. And fill the shelves they did.

While established brands such as New Balance, Adidas, and Puma certainly benefited from Nike's brand decline and retail pullback, two new brands that focused on running became big hits: Hoka and On. And another new brand arrived that focused on what to wear after your run.

Hoka: The Maximalist Running Shoe

Hoka was born in France and has super thick midsoles. A bit ugly and weird, this visible difference says you are serious about running, not style. The shoes were designed for running down steep mountains. In 2010, when Hoka's shoes debuted in the US market, minimalist "barefoot" running shoes were all the rage. Hoka went in the opposite direction.

Hoka's "maximalist" models had high-stack, thickly cushioned midsoles. But despite their thickness, they were extremely lightweight, and their rocker profile promoted a forward-balanced gait pattern. Hoka focuses on maximalism in a running shoe.

Hoka was purchased by Deckers Brands in 2013. Deckers owns other brands such as UGG and Teva. A portfolio of focused brands is a great corporate strategy. In 2023, Hoka drove corporate growth. Net sales increased by 58 percent to $1.41 billion.[3]

In 2024, Hoka sales increased 27.9 percent to $1.8 billion. Deckers' total gross margin was 56 percent, up from 50 percent in 2023.[4] They are on a roll.

On: Running on Clouds

Performance and technology were two things Nike put on the back burner, and On was on it. Yes, the brand name is On. It isn't great. But its technology was revolutionary.

Olivier Bernhard, a professional runner, six-time Ironman champion, and three-time world duathlon champion, had the radical idea for a shoe that felt like you were running on clouds. After his retirement in 2009, he pursued his dream and designed a shoe to deliver a running-on-clouds sensation. The project attracted the attention of like-minded engineers Caspar Coppetti and David Allemann. In 2010, the trio launched the brand in Zurich. A month later, a prototype of their shoe won the coveted ISPO Brandnew Award. Five months later On was on the shelves.[5]

Running on clouds is a powerful way to describe the running sensation they developed. The shoe creates both a cushioned landing as well as a firm take-off. They named their multidirectional cushioning system CloudTech. The system has a series of horizontal hollowed tubes (or "clouds") that offer stability each time the foot hits the ground. The clouds absorb the impact and then tighten to help push the foot off the ground. These clouds are visible too. The soles have holes in them.

The first shoe released was the Cloudracer, which gained notable attention when Swiss triathlete Nicola Spirig won the gold medal at the 2012 London Games in a thrilling photo finish.

Since then, On has become the shoe to run in and be seen in. In 2024, sales were $2.6 billion, and they tripled their net profit from the previous year.[6]

A great name can't make a bad strategy work. But a great strategy, combined with a weakened enemy, can make a name like On work. When you are the pioneer of running on clouds, there are advantages.

OOFOS: Active Recovery Footwear

With everybody running, OOFOS saw an opportunity to create a new type of shoe focused on active recovery after exercising. Running shoes like On are designed to offer rebound and energy return to spring you forward when you're running. OOFOS does the opposite. Its groundbreaking OOfoam technology absorbs shock. Its proprietary material absorbs 37 percent more impact than traditional foam footwear and is combined with a patented biomechanically engineered footbed that cradles arches and reduces ankle exertion by up to 47 percent.[7]

OOFOS created a new category folder in the mind. In 2011, it launched and promoted itself as the first active recovery shoe. Slogan: "Feel the OO, Feel Better, Faster." Recovery is a popular term in fitness circles. Naming the new category "active recovery shoe" was easily understood, even if the technology wasn't.

Brent Callaway, vice president of performance at Exos, teaches "Hard work + Rest = Success. We always tell our athletes, 'You can only train as hard as you can recover.' Recovery should be intentional. OOFOS reduce stress on the body."[8] Exos is an elite coaching facility that works with athletes to improve performance, including more than 200 Olympians, and is one of the many companies OOFOS has partnered with to promote its shoes.

While the enemy, Crocs, focuses on comfort, fashion, and jibbitz (the charms people adorn their Crocs with), OOFOS focuses on active recovery.

Skims: Inclusive Shapewear

Spanx started the twenty-first century shapewear revolution with its beige undergarments meant to suck, tuck, and hold you in. Spanx are a utility item worn discreetly under your clothing. The magic lies in nobody knowing you have it on. Fit and color are both key factors since the intent of Spanx and other shapewear is to fit close to the skin and blend in with your skin tone, so it won't be visible under light-colored or sheer clothing. "Nude" is a common word in fashion for a shade that resembles the human skin tone. However, as we know not all humans are beige.

Kim Kardashian personally felt frustrated by this and it led her to launch her own shapewear line in 2019, "When I was in my early 20s, there was only one color of shapewear, and it was this sort of light…it was not an actual skin tone, basically, but anyway it was a lot lighter than my skin. So I used to put my things in the sink and add tea bags or coffee to try to get the perfect realistic color. I couldn't really wear a new dress without something underneath it, to hold me up. So I had to dye them myself."[9]

Kardashian founded Skims with a focus on inclusivity of colors. She promotes Skims with cheeky marketing as celebratory shapeware that can just as easily be worn as sexy outerwear. Instead of hiding your body, Skims is about prioritizing body positivity. Who better than Kim Kardashian to promote that?

Kardashian, with her millions of followers and fans, could likely sell a fair amount of ice to the Eskimos. In fact, before launching her own brand, she attached her name and face to many products over the years from Carl's Jr. salads to Skechers to Midori liqueur to Silly Bandz bracelets. "We did every product you could imagine—from cupcake endorsements to a diet pill at the same time to sneakers or things that I didn't know enough about for them to be super-authentic to me," Kardashian told the *Los Angeles Times*.[10] Hiring a celebrity that has no credibility in using your product never works.

Kardashian is smart. She launched Skims, which is uniquely authentic to her, and started a movement. Skims had sales of $713 million in 2023, and her company is currently valued at $4 billion.[11] Skims is the shapewear of a new generation.

Skims resonates strongly with a diverse customer base often overlooked by fashion brands. For millions of women including me, Skims is a brand worth fighting for.

When You Focus, the Enemy Is Clear

Brandy Melville: One Size Fits Most

Brandy Melville is exclusively focused and isn't ashamed about it. While many brands have leaned into inclusivity by adding a wider range of sizes, Brandy did the opposite. Most of the clothes that Brandy Melville sells are "one size fits most" or small. The focus is affordable, trendy basics sold in one size. I recently stopped by a store in Chicago and witnessed a line down the street of teen girls and their moms waiting to get in. The security guard told me it is typical, especially on the weekends.

Before you get up in arms over the exclusive focus, there is a powerful strategy at play. Brandy Melville focuses on the pre-teen market. Before puberty hits, many young girls are more alike than you think. They also don't fit into traditional women's clothes that have ample room for boobs and hips. The one-size petite approach works particularly well for this target market.

The limited sizing is also a competitive advantage and makes for a relatively simple business. Smaller sizes require less material. Stocking the store is a breeze and there are no concerns of running out of popular sizes and being left with excess inventory.

Little is known about inner workings of the company; it was founded in Europe by Silvio Marsan, an Italian businessman. His sons run the American subsidiary. The chain has 50 stores globally with 41 in the United States. Annual sales totaled $212 million in 2023. This is, of course, is dwarfed by established teen apparel brand Abercrombie, which did $4.3 billion in sales in 2023.[12]

But how are you going to compete with Abercrombie and get attention for a new teen brand? It won't work to copy them. Brandy Melville has succeeded with a narrow focus on the petite girl's market. If you can launch a brand focused on plus-sizes only, why is it so controversial to do the opposite and focus on petite? An argument brought up in debates by many Brandy fans in online forums.

Brands can take things too far, and Brandy Melville has been dogged by accusations of discrimination for failing to hire female employees that were not young, thin, and white. A Canadian licensee alleged their license was terminated by the Marsans because the manager was "short" and "fat." The case is ongoing in the courts.

So far, the controversies have done little to dampen demand for the brand, but long term they need to tread carefully. Size exclusivity is one thing; only hiring and showcasing blonde, white teens is another and not cool.

Cuarto de Kilo: Two Ideas Aren't Better Than One

Two ideas are not better than one. Even if both ideas are super, it is best to focus only on one. We worked for Cuarto de Kilo and entrepreneur Alvaro Aguilar to help him narrow his focus and find his visual hammer.

At only 29 years old, Alvaro opened his first Cuarto de Kilo in Guadalajara, Mexico, in 2010. When we got hired in 2018, Cuarto de Kilo had 16 locations and was voted the number-one burger chain in Guadalajara's *Mural* newspaper for the second consecutive year with more than 50 percent of the votes.

Alvaro, a fan of positioning, wanted our advice on his brand. My father and I flew to Guadalajara to work with him. The location visits were impressive; the centerpiece of the restaurant is a rotating grill where the burgers are cooked over an open flame. Cuarto de Kilo's patented Gira-Grill is a clear and distinctive differentiator in the fast-food burger category.

Cuarto de Kilo is also known for their burger size. The name translates to "a quarter of a kilo," or about 0.55 pounds. The name makes it clear that customers will be getting a giant burger. Like, say, the "Quarter Pounder" offered by McDonald's.

The brand's logo and storefronts had the visual shown in Figure 6.1. It promoted the brand's two key and distinctive ideas.

The name, Cuarto de Kilo, promotes the oversized burger. And the visual plus the secondary name, Gira-Grill Burgers, promote the company's patented grill.

It seems logical to showcase both, but it's not. It causes confusion among customers and prospects. Simplicity and focus would help this brand a lot.

When You Focus, the Enemy Is Clear

Figure 6.1 The original logo of Cuarto de Kilo.
Source: Alvaro Aguilar / Amattia of America, INC.

Narrowing the Focus to One Idea

To focus, Alvaro would have to pick one. So which feature is the most important? The patented rotating Gira Grill, or the quarter-kilo weight?

That's the wrong question to ask. The right question is: Which feature will prospects instantly accept as a benefit?

It's the quarter-kilo weight. Consumers know that businesses can't falsify such things as the weight of the products they sell. Their competitors or the government would instantly sue them. When you say the burger is a quarter-kilo, it is instantly accepted by the mind.

The Gira Grill is harder to explain. It's not instantly obvious what it is, nor is it instantly differentiating in the mind.

We reviewed research Cuarto de Kilo had conducted that demonstrated this fact. Cuarto de Kilo's customers rated their favorite burger place as follows:

- Cuarto de Kilo: 42 percent
- Carl's Jr.: 38 percent
- McDonald's: 8 percent
- Burger King: 8 percent

Why was Carl's Jr. rated so highly? One reason might be the chain's logotype that focuses on "charbroiled burgers." So should Cuarto de Kilo focus on "charcoal broiling?" No. That's an idea that Carl's Jr. already owns in the mind. If the enemy is bigger and more well-known, focusing on the same idea is picking the wrong fight.

Finding a Visual Hammer and Battle Cry for Your Focus

When you focus your brand on a single benefit like oversize burgers, you can dramatize the idea both visually and verbally.

But just showing a burger visual doesn't communicate anything about its size. To know it's big, you need to show something else in relation to it.

In its famous Think Small advertisement, Volkswagen showed a VW Beetle next to 7'1" foot tall Wilt Chamberlain trying to squeeze into the front seat. Headline: "They said it could be done. It couldn't." VW's small size was clearly communicated next to the very tall Chamberlain.

Cuarto de Kilo needed a way to show how big their burgers were. We suggested a lion's wide-open mouth trying to fit the burger into it. The verbal slogan: "A feast for a beast." (See Figure 6.2.)

Figure 6.2 The new logo and visual hammer of Cuarto de Kilo. *Source:* Alvaro Aguilar / Amattia of America, INC.

After Alvaro had the final logo artwork created, he showed it to some friends and advisors. They responded, "Looks nice, but doesn't the lion look too angry?" Alvaro called us concerned. My dad, who had recently been on safari in Africa, answered, "Have you ever seen a lion eating? They are not smiling. The lion is perfect and authentic." Happy cartoon lions are fine for kiddy places; Cuarto de Kilo was for real lions.

A Problem: Long Wait Times

The average wait time at Cuarto de Kilo ranged from 15 minutes to as long as 40 minutes. To grow the brand and business, operations needed to be speedier. All you had to do was look at the menu to know what the problem was.

The menu had way too many items. There were 23 burgers on the menu. Offering so many options slowed down service and increased confusion in the consumers' minds. Picking a burger required too much thinking.

Our suggestion? Get rid of 19 burgers and focus only on four: (1) Bacon, (2) Classic, (3) Cheese, and (4) Guacamole.

These four items accounted for 51 percent of sales. Here are the percentages of 2017 food sales:

- Bacon: 17 percent
- Classic: 13 percent
- Cheese: 13 percent
- Guacamole: 8 percent

Many companies have similar looking sales figures. A few top sellers account for an overwhelming percentage of the business. Why not just focus on the winners?

Doing that takes courage. Most companies are driven by fear: "We can't drop the Honolulu; we will lose 6 percent of sales!" The reality is if the Honolulu is removed, customers will pick something else. Focusing on fewer items usually translates to improvements in speed and quality. We suggested dropping these nine burgers, which accounted for 34 percent of the food sales:

- Barbeque: 7 percent
- Honolulu: 6 percent
- Chorizo: 5 percent
- Mushroom: 4 percent
- Chipotle: 4 percent
- Shrimp: 3 percent
- Veggies: 2 percent
- Chicken: 2 percent
- Portobello: 1 percent

Lastly, we strongly recommended getting rid of all the half-burgers. These 13 half-quarters accounted for only 16 percent of food sales:

- Cheese: 4 percent
- Classic: 3 percent
- Bacon: 2 percent
- Guacamole: 1 percent
- Barbeque: 1 percent
- Honolulu: 1 percent
- Mushroom: 1 percent
- Chorizo: 1 percent
- Chipotle: 1 percent
- Veggies: 1 percent
- Shrimp: 0 percent
- Chicken: 0 percent
- Portobello: 0 percent

When You Focus, the Enemy Is Clear

Cuarto de Kilo is focused on big burgers. If they offer half-burgers, the consumer is faced with a mental dilemma. Feel gluttonous and order the whole burger, or be left hungry and order the half? Some choice. A lion would never eat just half a burger. A "feast for a beast" restaurant needs to act the same. Make the choice easy. And if customers don't finish it, they can take it home.

What About the Gira Spinning Grill?

The big burger idea is simple and instantly accepted. It is clearly and emotionally communicated in the visual hammer. The lion visual was enormously successful for Cuarto de Kilo. It is distinctive and theirs alone. And that is why it is the focus.

However, the spinning grill is just as important and powerful. It is the secondary idea that is best experienced in store. We suggested making the grill an even bigger part of the restaurant design. You go to Cuarto de Kilo for a big burger and then are wowed to see how it gets cooked on the spinning grill. It is hard to explain the grill idea until you see it and taste it. After you do, you have lots to tell your friends.

The grill also plays a key role in the brand's public relations strategy and benefits from third-party endorsement selling the idea. While the article might lead with the lion and big burger idea, the rest of the story talks about the grill.

Today, Cuarto de Kilo operates 35 restaurants across Mexico from Guadalajara to Mexico City, Puerto Vallarta, and Monterrey.

A Feast for a Beast Comes to America

After building the chain in Mexico, Alvaro's next dream was to take his brand to America. In 2023, he opened his first location in San Antonio, Texas.

While the burgers Cuarto de Kilo sells in America and the Gira-Grill they cook them on are exactly the same as in Mexico, the brand strategy had to be slightly adjusted.

The enemy and opportunity were different in the United States. There are several well-established better burger chains here already including Five Guys, Smashburger, and Cook Out. Just being big wasn't different enough.

In Mexico, Cuarto de Kilo is the hometown hero taking on the big American brands. In the United States, Cuarto de Kilo needed to emphasize its heritage and authenticity as a Mexican import. While their name is in Spanish, many brands in the United States use Spanish without being authentic brands. To establish the brand's credentials, PR would be critical in telling the Cuarto de Kilo story and spreading word of mouth.

A year after opening, the headline in the *San Antonio Express-News* read "Alvaro Aguilar imports Mexican-style hamburgers to San Antonio with Cuarto de Kilo chain."[13]

The article leads with a photo of Alvaro growling like a lion in front of a giant mural on the wall of a lion about to bite a burger. The spinning grill is also featured and pictured later and described as its "Artisan Made-in-Mexico Gira-Grill, patented to Cuarto de Kilo, a Mesquite Mexican burger restaurant."

In Mexico, the focus is big burgers. In America, the focus is on big Mexican burgers. "We want to start a new category called Mexican authentic burgers," Aguilar said.

Again, the grill concept is important but takes too much time to explain and distinguish from other brands such as Burger King's flame-broiled taste or Cook Out's home-barbeque flavor. Instead of trying to communicate a spinning grill nobody has heard of, they focused on the mesquite. Mesquite is instantly understood as premium and something most other brands can't claim. Plus, it is alterative with Mexican. When driving down the street, you see the name: Cuarto de Kilo; the visual hammer: lion eating the burger; the slogan: a feast for a beast; and the category: Mesquite Mexican Burgers. Pretty compelling pitch to pull over for.

A Focus for Nonprofits

Nonprofits also benefit from a narrow focus. Doing good is done better when you focus. When you communicate what you do in a specific way, it drives emotion, support, and action.

Tunnel to Towers: Mortgage-Free Homes

After facing a tragedy, many individuals pursue making a difference in the world by starting a nonprofit. September 11, 2001, was a tragic day in US history. A total of 2,977 victims were killed in the terrorist attacks. Frank Siller's little brother Stephen was one of them.

Stephen Siller was a New York City firefighter assigned to Brooklyn's Squad 1. On September 11, he had just finished his shift and was on his way to play golf with his brothers when he heard on his scanner of a plane hitting the North Tower of the World Trade Center. Stephen immediately went back to the firehouse, grabbed his gear, and headed to the Brooklyn Battery Tunnel, but the tunnel had already been closed for security reasons. Determined to carry out his first responder duties, Stephen strapped 60 pounds of gear to his back and raced on foot through the tunnel to the Twin Towers, where he met up with other members of Squad 1. The first responders were heroic that day, and sadly Stephen and many others with him lost their lives fighting to save others.

When Frank got the call saying his brother was among the missing firefighters, he and his family were devastated. A short time later Frank suggested starting a nonprofit to honor what Stephen and others did that fateful day. They called it the Tunnel to Towers Foundation.

In September 2002, the first annual Tunnel to Towers 5K Run & Walk was held. It symbolizes Stephen's final steps from the Battery Tunnel to the Twin Towers and pays homage to the 343 FDNY firefighters, law enforcement officers, and thousands who lost their lives on 9/11. The annual T2T 5K began with 1,500 people and has since included over 500,000 participants.

Tunnel to Towers could have written a mission statement like many nonprofits do: "To honor and empower first responders and veterans through programs and services." But they didn't. They were very specific.

The Tunnel to Towers mission is to provide mortgage-free homes to our nation's heroes and the families they leave behind.

So far, T2T has raised $1 billion dollars and provided 1,500 mortgage-free homes. They have focused even further and are building a community of smart homes in Land O' Lakes, Florida, named the "Let Us Do Good Village." The village is a first-of-its-kind T2T community of nearly 100 mortgage-free homes provided to catastrophically injured veterans and first responders, as well as America's Gold Star and fallen first responder families. The impact of the village goes far beyond just the families living there; it is a visible centerpiece of the organization's mission and impact.

The foundation started by assisting first responders and has carried on that tradition to assist policemen, US Marshals, Gold Star Families, and others killed in the line of duty. But they do so while still maintaining a focus on homes.

Foundation organizers have reached out to the public for donations of $11 a month for the new "In the Line of Duty" program, which helps fund three housing programs. Gold Star Family Home Program recipient Nancy Gass summed it up like this: "Tunnel to Towers is changing the world, one heart and one house at a time."[14]

Tunnel to Towers' current Charity Watch rating is A+. In 2023, they raised $373 million with 93% of fundraising dollars directly funding programs.[15]

To learn more: https://T2T.org

The Smasherson Foundation: Radiation Calendars

Emerson Podojil was a healthy and active 10-year-old girl. She loved to make people laugh and lit up any room she walked in with her wit, energy, and smile.

In August 2018, after several days of headaches, vomiting, and fatigue, she was taken to the Emergency Department of Children's Healthcare of Atlanta. The ER doctor figured it was just a late summer cold but to be safe ordered a head CT scan. Within 30 minutes of the scan came the heart-breaking news. They found a mass in the center of Emerson's brain. One week later little Emerson underwent a six-hour surgery to remove the mass. While the surgery was a success, the pathology revealed Grade IV Diffuse Midline Glioma with a mutation called H3K27M. The prognosis was bleak, but Emerson, her parents, and sister were strong. Emerson began what would be multiple sets of radiation treatments to try to keep the tumor at bay. In the end, the cancer proved to be relentless, and Emerson died 10 months later in June 2019.

I was at Emerson's funeral. Her parents are dear friends. Her father Jeff's eulogy was so beautiful but one that no father should ever have to give. Soon after her passing, the family founded a foundation in 2020 in her honor to fund research for Children's Healthcare of Atlanta Neuro-Oncology's team as well as provide emotional support to children and families of all pediatric cancers. They needed a name for the foundation and a focus.

First, the name: Throughout treatment, her family always referred to Emerson's tumor as a squishy little ball that needed to be smashed to get rid of it. They often talked about smashing that ball. So, they named the foundation Smasherson (Smash & Emerson), which was a fitting name to honor her fighting spirit. Smasherson's mission would be to smash and eradicate this devastating disease.

The focus: While the foundation's goal was raising money for research, there are lots of organizations with that same goal. How could Smasherson be different? What could it be known for? The answer lies in focusing on something specific like Tunnel to Towers did with mortgage-free homes for heroes. Focusing on one specific and unique thing that was meaningful and memorable.

One of the most special gifts Emerson received during treatment was a Radiation Countdown Calendar, which is like the Advent Calendars you see during the holidays. A Radiation Countdown Calendar is a set of small gifts that children get to open after each radiation session. For Emerson, this was incredibly important and impactful. It gave her something to look forward to after treatment. It also allowed her to see her progress along the way. Her family decided this would be the best gift the foundation could give to other children and their families.

Smasherson is focused on creating Radiation Countdown Calendars for children being treated with radiation. The calendars are carefully curated and made especially for each child based on their likes and interests.

They have partnered with Emory's Proton Therapy Center and provide every child undergoing radiation a calendar. Smasherson delivers 200 calendars a year to children in treatment, which equates to over 6,000 gifts a year.

Consistent feedback from the doctors, nurses, and families is that the radiation calendar is often the only thing that will get the child into treatment. Smasherson is filling a gap and creating a positive experience for other children and their families during cancer treatment.

Lastly, the logo: The pig. Emerson loved pigs. It is distinctive and unique to her. The group of friends Emerson has had since kindergarten and who never left her side during her treatment became the foundation's junior board of directors and known as the Piggy Pals. They represent what true friendship and the bond of sisterhood means. The Piggy Pals and many other community volunteers work hard to add love to every radiation calendar they create.

To learn more, visit https://smasherson.org/.

Kate's Club: Grief Is Good, Even for Kids

Kate's Club is the club you don't want to join, but if you need to, you are forever grateful that the club exists. One in 11 children in the United States experience the death of a parent or sibling by age 18.[16] Kate Atwood was one of them.

Kate was 12 years old when she lost her mother to breast cancer. After her mom died, grief was her number-one enemy. Like many do, she firmly tucked it away and marched on. To others she looked to be thriving, and everybody assumed she was fine. She did well in school, excelled in sports, and even was elected class president. While she was an outward achiever, inside she suffered with shame, sadness, and anxiety. She did everything except to grieve.

While in college she volunteered at a bereavement camp on a whim. One night a leader suggested she share her story with the young campers. Kate had never talked about her mom or her grief. She discovered the importance of sharing her story and being around others who had experienced the same thing. That night changed her perspective around grief. It should not be filled with shame, avoidance, or isolation. Grief is something we are meant to go through together.

It inspired her to start Kate's Club three years later. Kate was 23 years old, living in a new city, and had no money. But she was filled with a conviction to change the world for grieving children. To get started she raised $1,000 during a bar night fundraiser for her new nonprofit.

The first official Kate's Club outing involved Kate and a few volunteers taking six grieving children to a bowling alley. Since then, the organization has helped more than 10,000 grieving kids, teens, young adults, and their families throughout Georgia. Kate's Club is now available in school systems across the state and has recently expanded to four new regional centers outside of Georgia.

Grief isn't something many people want to talk about. Early on a friend reminded Kate, "The top three fears most people have in life are public speaking, death, and asking for money. You are doing all three."[17] It's not going to be easy.

Before she had an actual clubhouse, Kate would meet new families at a coffee shop. One day while coming to meet three young girls who lost their father, she heard the youngest say to her sister, "Well, she doesn't look like what I thought she'd look like."

23-year-old Kate replied, "Well, what did you think I was going to look like?"

"Old and wearing black," said the little girl.

At Kate's Club grief is not the enemy. The *misperceptions* of grief are the enemy.

- Grief should be personal and hidden. Wrong. Grief is best shared with others.
- Grief is for old people. Wrong. Grief is for everyone, and all ages.
- Children are too young to grieve, so it is best not to bring it up. Wrong. All children grieve.
- If you can't see the grief, then the child must be okay. Wrong. All children need grief support.

If a kid falls and breaks their arm, we don't just wait and see how it works out, if the bones heal on their own, and deal with it later if it becomes an issue. We immediately get the kid help. Why don't we do this for grief?

Kate's Club focuses on the mantra that "Grief is Good." Not that it's easy or wanted. But when it arrives, especially in childhood, grief becomes your lifelong journey. And that journey will be a better one when it is filled with connections, not avoidance.

A world where grief is good is not a scary one. It is a healthy and human one. It is a connected one. Kate's Club is a place for grieving children to connect with others and grow through their grief experience. Thanks to Kate's Club, children can experience a world where grief is good.

To learn more, visit https://www.katesclub.org/.

Nobody ever knows how they will respond to grief or tragedy. Life can change in an instant. If you are driven to change the world, we need more of this. Just remember: to be successful in helping others and to bring attention to your cause, your branding and focus will go a long way in helping you succeed. Use it wisely.

Core Concepts: When You Focus, the Enemy Is Clear

- A focus is necessary to build a strong brand.
- A focus will make the enemy clear.
- A focus will guide long-term decision making.
- Two ideas are not better than one; focus on one.

Chapter 7

An Enemy Fuels Debate

We all love a debate. Debates tap into our instincts to take sides and give people a sense of identity and belonging. Politics and sports are commonplace for debates. Democrats vs. Republicans. Green Bay Packers vs Chicago Bears. Strategic enemies fuel great brand debates. Mac vs. PC. Dunkin' vs Starbucks. These rivalries engage audiences, create buzz and reinforce each brand's unique value. Over time most categories become dominated by two opposing brands; these brands benefit from being the most discussed and debated.

■ ■ ■

When there are two easily understood and defined options it kicks off a debate. The conflict and contrast between two brands drive engagement and creates tension that our brains find stimulating. It literally fires up your brain.

Too many sides, however, make having a debate impossible. Remember when the Republicans had 10 candidates on the stage in 2015? It works best when two sides debate in politics as well as in branding. Sure, you may have a few fringe parties, but eventually most categories become dominated by two leading brands.

A debate will fuel interest in the category as well as the brands that stand on both sides. No one brand is for everyone, there is always room for an alternative. Slow vs fast. Big vs. small. Complex vs. simple. Cheap vs. expensive. Square vs. round.

A debate motivates everybody to have an opinion and pick a side. Consumers love to have an opinion. Experts love to have an opinion. The media love to write about opinions. Your mother most certainly loves to have an opinion. She would also like you to text her back. Make sure to say you love her.

Strong opinions fire people up. Without controversy, without differences, there is no debate. The danger for brands is being too bland and boring. Not standing for anything gets you ignored. It is better to be talked about, even if not everybody agrees with your position. Maybe one day they will.

Word of mouth is a key driver of brand success; a debate gives people something specific to talk about and take a stand on. As a brand, you need to arm your supporters with simple facts and arguments. The goal is to build up an army that will promote, amplify, and further your cause.

The Internet has become a hotbed of lively discussions and heated debates. Comparisons between two opposing brands have become a new category of content on Reddit, YouTube, TikTok, and more. Some titles of posts include:

- "Shopify vs. Amazon: The age old question"
- "Mrs. Fields vs. Crumbl Cookies Taste Test | Food Feuds"

- "The Great Debate: Dunkin' vs Starbucks?"
- "Duolingo vs. Babbel: What I learned by comparing them"

When consumers are faced with a choice between two brands, which source gives them the most useful and trusted info? The brand websites or the Reddit debate on which to pick? Reddit's third-party endorsements cut to the chase of what the true differences are. Then lets you decide which is right for you.

While brands have seconds to make an impression, debates lead to more detailed discussions allowing your brand story to shine. Your story energizes consumers to see your brand as something worth fighting for.

The Great Luggage Debate: Hard vs. Soft

The debate between hard and soft luggage has been going on for decades. The pendulum swing between which side is winning is largely generational. Many in the new generation don't want a suitcase that looks like the one their parents owned. This opens opportunities for new brands to emerge.

If your brand is established on the soft or hard side, there isn't much you really should do except to stick to your position and ride the ups and downs of fashion. Strangely enough, many kids think the luggage their grandparents have is classic and cool.

I have picked three dominant brands to represent the great luggage debate. Each brand has a unique story of how they pioneered a new category, used a visual hammer, and have remained consistent. These brands engage consumers and have fueled many debates over which bag is best.

On the Hard Side: Rimowa

Rimowa is the pioneer of hard aluminum luggage. In 1898, Paul Morszeck started crafting custom suitcases made of leather-coated plywood and cardboard in Cologne, Germany. As business grew,

Paul specialized in smaller and more durable boxes and cases for his cosmopolitan clientele.

However, it was the second generation of the family that made a pivotal decision that led to the company's iconic status. As the legend goes, a fire in the 1930s destroyed everything in the company's factory but aluminum. This led Paul's son Richard to proclaim it as the brand's future focus, ending the brand's use of wood materials forever.

It was the dawn of aviation, and duralumin, as the special alloy is technically named, was discovered outside of Cologne. Duralumin played a key role in aviation milestones such as the world's first all-metal aircraft. Richard saw duralumin as perfect for suitcases as it was lightweight, durable, and corrosion-resistant. His craftsmen dubbed it as having Persönlichkeit or "personality." It was different, distinctive, and cool.[1]

As part of his new focus on aluminum suitcases, Richard renamed the company to Rimowa using the first two letters of his name (**RI**chard **MO**rszeck) and the word (**WA**renzeichen), which means "trademark" in German. Morszeck would have been the typical way to brand the company, but Rimowa is better. Simple, unique, plus easy to say and spell. Names matter.

The final touch of the brand's distinctiveness was added in the 1950s when Rimowa added grooves to the aluminum. The inspiration for the grooved design came from the corrugated fuselage of German-made Junkers F-13 planes and has made Rimowa one of the world's most recognizable luggage brands.[2] In 2016, Rimowa joined the LVMH group, which has expanded the brand globally while still maintaining its focus.

When you see a Rimowa bag, you recognize it instantly. In a sea of black bags, Rimowa's silver bag with its grooved design stands out. When I see another traveler with a Rimowa like me, we are instantly connected. And often strike up a conversation about our bags and travels. We are part of the same tribe.

As a 125-year-old brand, Rimowa has been wise to reinforce and defend the brand and it's hard side position with advertising. Rimowa's slogan is "Engineered for Life" and uses the visual of its iconic aluminum case.[3] Advertising works best when you have a visual hammer that is established in the mind. They also continue to generate PR on bags themselves. In 2025, Rimowa put a collection of vintage suitcases for sale on its US website that were covered with dents, scratches, old stickers, and luggage tags. The cost ranged from $600 to $1,000. Owners of Rimowa suitcases see the worn and torn look as a badge of honor.

On the Soft Side: Tumi

Tumi is the pioneer of durable soft-side luggage. In 1975, Charlie Clifford returned from the Peace Corps and started a luggage company. He named it Tumi after the ceremonial knife the Peruvians used for sacrifices. It wasn't until the 1980s that Tumi established the brand in the mind of consumers with the release of its legendary soft-sided carry-on garment bag in ballistic nylon. The extremely durable and sleek black-on-black aesthetic is the visual hammer and signature of the brand. Tumi has continued to innovate in technology and boasts more than 125 patents on such features as the omega closure system, swivel "P" handle, and integrated wheel assembly.[4]

Here is the thing: while Tumi has expanded the line under more recent owners, it is wise to continue to promote the original. When they promote their new aluminum suitcases, they look like an imitator to Rimowa, which they are. Tumi's brand anchor is its black signature soft ballistic material. To be thought of as authentic requires you to be first and then to consistently promote your visual. Authenticity is at the heart of success, and Tumi in black has it in spades, which is why Samsonite spent $1.8 billion in cash to purchase Tumi in 2016.[5] Let's just hope they don't do too much damage via expansion.

Tumi recently launched a line of men's and women's fragrances and promoted them as smelling like a worldly adventure and capturing the "true essence of wanderlust."[6] I have owned Tumi bags for years and taken them all over the world. The last thing I want to smell like is my luggage. Tumi isn't a "lifestyle" or "fashion" brand; it is a terrific, classic, iconic black ballistic bag.

The Hard Side Newcomer: Away Luggage

With the success of Tumi, soft-sided luggage had its heyday from the mid-1980s into the new century. I remember rolling my eyes when my in-laws came to visit us in 1999 with their hard-sided luggage. So uncool.

While Rimowa had fans at the high-end, most luggage was still sold on the soft side. The arrival of Away Luggage changed all that. It was a new brand focused exclusively on affordable hard-sided luggage for the tech-savvy millennial traveler.

After Jen Rubio's suitcase broke and all her stuff poured out on to the floor of an airport in Switzerland, she decided to do something. She called her former colleague at Warby Parker, Steph Korey, and the two cooked up the idea of a durable hard-shell suitcase sold direct-to-consumer with a built-in battery pack for charging your phone.

In 2015, the two secured $150,000 from friends and family, hired an industrial designer, and headed to China to find a factory willing to take a chance on two young women with a dream.

By Christmas, Away's online marketing was ready to roll, but the bags were not. Not wanting to miss the giving season, they offered the bags for pre-order and started a targeted social media campaign. Consumers felt like they were getting in early on the next big thing, which as we now know they were. In February 2016, Away's first product, the Carry-On, was shipped to customers. It was a hit.[7]

But it wasn't all Instagram ads and social influencer postings that drove the brand's success. The Away Carry-On was also a major PR success story. *Vogue* called it "The Perfect Carry-On." *People* dubbed it "the little black dress of luggage."

Away is known for its hard-sided polycarbonate suitcases with sleek design and practical features. While selling luggage direct was unique, the product was not. Away was not the first polycarbonate suitcase on the market.

Would you believe Rimowa was pioneer of polycarbonate? It was. Rimowa launched the very first polycarbonate suitcase in 2000. Using polycarbonate was a major innovation that offered a highly durable material that was extremely lightweight. Rimowa was smart; the company made its polycarbonate bags look the same as its original aluminum bags. Rimowa's aluminum bag is still the brand anchor and visual hammer.

After Rimowa, lots of companies added products made from polycarbonate to their line from Samsonite to American Tourister to Delsey. But until Away, no brand took ownership of the polycarbonate category in the mind of the consumer. They were all line-extensions under the main brand.

Away succeeded by focusing on polycarbonate only and being the choice of a new generation. But if Rimowa was technically the first, how could Away differentiate and not be perceived as an imitator? The answer was simple: Rimowa's grooves are vertical. Away's are horizontal. Away put its lines in the opposite direction. Brilliant and visible from across the terminal. It often doesn't take much to be distinctive, sometimes just lines going in the other direction.

As the choice of a new generation, Away has recently expanded into more colors, especially limited-edition ones like pink, green, yellow and purple. Tumi in wild colors makes no sense, but colors are authentic to Away. Reminds me of the colorful iMacs of the 1990s.

The Great Online Shopping Debate: Amazon vs. Shopify

Going up against an 800-pound gorilla isn't for the faint hearted. The good news is everybody loves a David versus Goliath story. The bad news is that Goliath usually wins.

Many online retailers have tried to compete with Amazon. Amazon has destroyed most of them, including Buy.com, eToys.com, Webvan, and many more.

When you go up against a behemoth like Amazon, you obviously can't attack them where they are strong. It is best to start with a niche too small for them to bother with. And remember that in every great strength, there is some element of weakness to exploit.

That's what Shopify did. Today Shopify is worth $148 billion and is the second-largest e-commerce company outside of China. Second, of course, to Amazon. But how did Shopify succeed? They created a simple way for small companies to set up their own online store with all the bells and whistles. Most importantly, Shopify gave owners the opportunity to sell directly to consumers via their own website instead of being a third-party vendor on Amazon.

The Shopify story begins in 2004 when three friends with a shared passion for snowboarding decided to launch an online store to sell snowboarding equipment. The brand name, Snowdevil, came easily. Setting up the site was more challenging. Running an online store required them to build and host a site, process payments, and manage orders and customer service. While there were individual products available to solve these issues, there wasn't a one-stop simple solution. Luckily one of the three friends, Tobias Lutke, was a passionate software developer who set out to build what they needed: a unified e-commerce system.

Snowdevil's success led to inquiries from other retailers about their technology and how they could use it too. This was the spark for what would become Shopify. The friends quickly realized their future was not in selling snowboarding equipment; it was in selling their software solution.

The original brand name was Jaded Pixel. While a creative and techy name, the brand's prospects were not computer geeks; they were store owners looking for simplicity. So, they changed the name to Shopify, which does a much better job of communicating simplicity for shop owners.[8]

Shopify was built on an open-source template, meaning it allowed advanced users to customize their own storefronts with ease. This belief in an open approach led them to launch the Shopify App Store where developers could build and sell their own apps to users. This greatly accelerated the number of tailor-made Shopify solutions available for marketing, social media, SEO, shipping, localization, design, and much more.

From the beginning Amazon has been wildly focused on the customer. Remember that in every strength, there is an opportunity to stand for the opposite. Amazon's customer-friendly focus is often to the detriment of the sellers on the platform. Shopify, on the other hand, is entirely focused on the seller and making it as easy as possible for them to do business. Shopify is the merchant hero.

However, when Shopify tried to go up against Amazon in delivery, it was a disaster. Delivery is an area where Amazon excels; competing would require huge capital investments in logistics, delivery, and warehousing. And even with enough investment, competing with Amazon in delivery was a losing battle. Shopify quickly exited the strategy after a year. They refocused on being a purely digital player for sellers.

Why would Shopify even attempt to go after the delivery market? Because their merchants asked them to add the service. Callie's Hot Little Biscuits was one of Shopify's first 100 customers. The owner mentioned how hard it was to manage a lot of orders and figure out the cheapest delivery method each day. It is a typical scenario; most companies gather feedback from customers and then add additional features and services. This is why knowing when to say no is so important. Expanding the brand to delivery was a bad idea. Luckily, they quickly figured it out and told Callie "No" to adding logistics.[9]

Today, if you are a business selling products online, the first thing you decide is to go with Amazon or Shopify. The brand is firmly established as the alternative to Amazon. There are thousands of articles, videos, and posts debating on which one is better. Everybody has an opinion and this debate benefits both brands.

In addition, Shopify itself is a content powerhouse. Shopify's blog is packed with success stories, ideas, how-tos, and more[10], cementing their commitment to store merchants.

The Great Lodging Debate: Hotels vs. Airbnb

Airbnb revolutionized lodging with its rent-a-room concept as an alternative to a hotel room. The name stands for "Air Bed and Breakfast." It started back in October 2007 when three friends in San Francisco got the bright idea to rent out their living room to conference goers who couldn't find a hotel room and let them sleep on air mattresses. If you have ever been to a big conference in San Fransico, you know what a great idea this is. Hotel rooms are outrageously expensive if you can find one.

An Enemy Fuels Debate

The initial focus was on Airbnb "hosts" willing to rent out a spare room to make some extra money and Airbnb "guests" looking for cheap lodging. Since then, the category has evolved and expanded. Today Airbnb is the leading platform for lodging of all types from a room to a house to a villa.

There are even real estate investors who have made Airbnb-ing their full-time job by buying and hosting properties. And with more than 8 million active global listings,[11] you can find a wide range of Airbnbs to stay at from basic to exotic.

Airbnb isn't just for cheap travelers anymore; it is for all travelers. The average price of an Airbnb in North America is $163 a night[12] versus $171 for a hotel.[13] The average price for a budget hotel is $93.

It is the great travel debate of our time. Do we Airbnb or stay in a hotel?

Late to the Debate: VRBO

VRBO (Vacation Rental by Owner) was founded in 1995 by David Clouse. He created a website to rent out his ski home in Breckenridge, Colorado. Websites were just beginning at the time, so VRBO was the first of its kind. From that one ski home, VRBO now includes more than 2 million homes to rent around the world.[14]

HomeAway was founded in 2004 with a plan to acquire vacation rentals companies and merge them into a single marketplace. They launched the HomeAway brand in 2006 and that same year acquired VRBO. But they never merged VRBO and HomeAway and operated the brands separately.

Multiple brands are an effective strategy for large companies looking to expand into new categories. However, multiple brands are usually a terrible idea for entrepreneurs or smaller companies competing with strong competitors.

In 2015, Expedia Group, one of the world's leading online travel agencies, was looking to get into the category Airbnb was dominating. So, they bought HomeAway for $3.9 billion. To take on Airbnb, Expedia knew they needed to focus on one brand, one position, one name. HomeAway was too generic. V-R-B-O was too long and difficult to say. Launching a totally new name would be risky and costly. VRBO had authenticity and a rich history. HomeAway did not. So, in 2019, Expedia shut down HomeAway and rebranded VRBO as Vrbo to be pronounced as Ver-boh—a pronunciation loyal fans had been using for years.

Then they upped the marketing and called out Airbnb as the enemy. Unlike Airbnb, Vrbo has never listed properties where guests stay with hosts. Its focus is on whole home vacation rentals only. Airbnb offers both.

In 2024, Vrbo started running ads featuring former Alabama head coach Nike Saban as a gruff and grizzly host. Saban, known as a disciplinarian in winning seven national football championships, is the perfect person to embody a nightmarish rental host. Saban greets his guest by reviewing his big binder of rules. "No showers longer than five minutes; this isn't a spa. No games, no fun. Two flush maximum per bathroom visit." Then we see the couple in the hot tub along with Saban, who reminds them, "You guys got about 10 minutes. . .cause this is Daddy time in the tub." A line he apparently ad-libbed. It ends with the reminder to experience the freedom of host-free vacation rentals, only at Vrbo.[15]

The message was perfect, but the timing was not. Had this aggressive campaign and message been launched in 2010 instead of 2024, perhaps things could have been different. Today, after nearly two decades, Airbnb has evolved in the market and the mind from their host-on-property roots.

Recently, in a ridiculous attempt to seek attention, Vrbo put up a billboard outside of Airbnb's San Francisco offices that poked the bear: "Think of us as Airbnb's hotter, cooler, friendlier, long-lost twin that never has hosts." Advertising is effective only if it reinforces something already in the mind. Airbnb called the stunt "desperate" and said the campaign just gives Airbnb "more visibility."[16] I couldn't agree more.

The Great Toothbrush Debate: Oral-B vs. Sonicare

When it comes to brushing your teeth, switching from a manual toothbrush to an electric one is a good move. Electric toothbrushes make it easier to remove plaque, reduce bacteria, and polish teeth while protecting your enamel, and built-in timers keep you going the whole two minutes.

Once you decide to go electric, there are two brands that dominate the category: Sonicare, the pioneer and specialist, and Oral-B, the generalists that build its electric brand with a different head. The head-to-head battle has been raging for years, fueling debate in the media, dentist offices, and bathrooms around the world. Everybody has an opinion, which benefits both brands and drives interest in the category itself.

It all started with research at the University of Washington that found that exposure to acoustic energy lessened the ability of common oral bacteria to adhere to teeth. David Giuliani, an entrepreneur and electrical engineer, met with the Washington professors in 1987, and together they formed a company to create a toothbrush using this new sonic technology.

Sonicare Advance, the world's first sonic toothbrush, was launched in 1992. It caused quite a stir and garnered a ton of PR. By the year 2000, Sonicare had $175 million in sales and was the number-one brand of electric toothbrushes in terms of dollar share with 46 percent.[17] That same year Philips, the Dutch conglomerate, acquired them.

What do you suppose they did next? Of course, they added the Philips name to the package. Not in a small way either. The Philips name and Sonicare name carried equal weight. Two names are not better than one. Sonicare was the toothbrush and the generic for the category itself. Adding the Philips name in such large print served no purpose except to inflate corporate ego. Philips, while a huge company, was relatively unknown in the United States except for maybe light bulbs. To improve their brand image is probably why they slapped their name on the product. But it made no sense in the mind. The consumer wanted a Sonicare and now that name was smaller and only half as important on the package.

As the pioneer and specialist, Sonicare still holds the edge, but geez. While Philips was wise to buy the brand, they were foolish to add their name on the front of the package. The company would have gotten PR credit in the business community for Sonicare's success without confusing consumers by using two names on the package.

Oral-B is the generalist, using what is called a "Master Brand" strategy. Meaning they use one brand on everything including manual toothbrushes, electric toothbrushes, toothpaste, mouthwash, floss, and more. Basically, a nicer term for line-extension.

The brand started out as just a toothbrush. A California periodontist, Robert Hutson, designed and patented his "Hutson Toothbrush" in 1950. He continued to innovate and by 1958 registered a patent for a "mouthbrush" with numerous, fine, soft, flat-ended nylon bristles. During the filling process, Huston claimed that this brush was less abrasive to tooth enamel and better for massaging the gums than other brushes available at the time.[18] The brand name he created was Oral-B, short for "Oral-Brush." The first product was the Oral-B 60 because it had 60 tufts. This was an incredible innovation that led to a lot of PR. In the 1960s Hutson sold the business, it was bought by Gillette in 1984, and it is now part of Procter & Gamble.

Oral-B is a weaker name compared to Sonicare. While a well-known name in oral care, it doesn't stand for anything after so many years of line-extensions. How can it position itself against Sonicare, the original, the leader, and what many assume to be the best? In the mind, the leader is always perceived to be the best.

Oral-B saying it was better was unlikely to work with consumers or the media. Instead, they focused on being different. Sonicare's brush has a standard oval head like a traditional toothbrush. Oral-B's brush, on the other hand, has a round head.

While there are many technical specifications to both brushes, including rotations and more, the simple visual difference of the head is what sets them apart. This difference fuels the debate between the two in articles and discussions about the brands. When you can lead with a visual difference, it gives the media and consumers something to talk about.

Round is different, and different is good. But Oral-B should hammer the point even harder on why it is better. Oral-B electric toothbrushes are round for a reason. Round tools are what dentists use.

An Enemy Fuels Debate

A key part of both brands' strategy are dentist and hygienist referrals; both send representatives frequently to encourage sales. Last time I was at the dentist I asked my hygienist which brand was best. She answered using either Sonicare or Oral-B is better than brushing manually. But then she pointed out the difference of the head shapes. "Oral-B's round head is the same I am cleaning your teeth with today. All our tools are round; I think it is better." That's the strategy that hammers the enemy; Oral-B is the more professional-looking brush.

The Great Debate: USA vs. China

The United States and China are the world's two largest economies. When it comes to the great debate in branding, the world is waiting to see what Chinese companies will emerge to take on American brands globally. The assumption is that China's leading brands have great potential as global brands. And they do.

American companies have been going global since the mid-twentieth century and dominate when it comes to building global brands. According to the 2024 Interbrand list of the top global brands, 53 are from the United States including the top four brands: Apple, Microsoft, Amazon, and Google. Two Chinese brands recently cracked the list: Xiaomi at #87 and Huawei at #93.[19]

The story is interesting because everyone is waiting to see what will happen next. What Chinese companies are next to take on the global markets with their brands? Xiaomi and Huawei are potentially the tips of the iceberg.

The opportunity is great, but it won't be easy. In the early 1990s, many pundits predicted that Japanese companies would win the global branding battle. The Japanese rising sun was expected to roll over America. It never happened. While Japan is still the fourth largest economy in the world, apart from Toyota, Honda, and Nissan, they have not been very successful in building global brands. Why? Most companies in Japan sell a wide range of products all under a single brand name.

Decades ago, Japan's electronic industry dominated world markets. No longer. Line extension has weakened companies such as Toshiba, Fujitsu, Sony, Panasonic, Hitachi, and NEC. Sony, once a global superstar, has recently rebounded but mainly based on the success of its narrowly focused PlayStation brand.

China would be wise to study Japan's mistakes. Chinese companies should be wary of using line extension over focus, especially as they go global. What may work in the domestic market is less likely to work globally where you face even more specialized competitors.

Chinese brands also need to carefully consider the brand names they use when going global. As a general rule, we say global brand names work best when they sound right in English. They don't need to be English words, just relatively easy to say and spell if you know some English. English is the world's most popular second language and the one used in business, science, aviation, and diplomacy between people who speak different languages.

English and Chinese are vastly different languages. English uses a phonetic alphabet consisting of 26 letters that represent sounds. Chinese uses a logographic writing system, where each character represents a word or a meaningful part of a word. The number of characters in Chinese is vast, with thousands needed to be literate. It is interesting: the Chinese write in pictures; English uses words. But trying to translate the sounds of these characters into letters isn't easy. And names like Xiaomi and Huawei are difficult to read and pronounce for English speakers. While these brands have done well despite the tough names, there is a better strategy they could have used. The better strategy is to use a new name globally.

The TikTok of China: Douyin

TikTok has already become a global giant. ByteDance dominates the Chinese and the global market using two brands and one visual hammer. Here is the history.

Before Douyin, there was Musical.ly, which invented the genre of short, vertical, lip-sync phone videos in 2014. Users picked from a database of songs, recorded themselves for 1 to 15 seconds lip-syncing, added preset filters and effects, and then shared it with the world. It was a narrow focus that gained instant popularity with teenagers. By 2016, Musical.ly had 90 million users.[20] Musical.ly was founded in Shanghai but also had an office in California.

ByteDance was a Chinese app factory. The company operated more than a dozen apps with shared recommendation engines and user data. After noticing the success of Musical.ly, they rapidly developed a similar app in 200 days. They launched Douyin in 2016. Within a year Douyin had 100 million users.

Douyin's founder, Zhang Yiming, was not satisfied with only domestic expansion for the brand. He is famously quoted as saying, "China is home to only one-fifth of Internet users globally. If we don't expand on a global scale, we are bound to lose to peers eyeing the four-fifths. So, going global is a must."[21]

In 2017, ByteDance launched a global version of the Douyin platform. While Douyin is a great name in Chinese, it's hard to pronounce and doesn't have any meaning in English. Instead, Yiming named the app TikTok outside of China. One brand, two names. In Chinese, the name isn't really Douyin, it is these characters: 抖音. The characters translate to "shaking sound." The letters "Douyin" are Pinyin, which uses the Roman alphabet to transcribe Mandarin pronunciations. Pinyin is widely used for typing Chinese characters and as a guide for Chinese pronunciation. It allows nonspeakers to pronounce Chinese words without needing to learn Chinese characters. Instead of teaching the world what Douyin means in Chinese, they simply used TikTok, which is instantly understood by English speakers.

Important to note: The two brands use the same logo and visual hammer: the music note. This visual unifies the two brands globally as one. It is a strategy more Chinese brands should consider.

TikTok had a significant enemy in Musical.ly, the original video app. At the time, Musical.ly had momentum, great PR, and more than 200 million followers. TikTok had two choices. One, focus on competing with Musical.ly and try to position themselves as different. Or two, buy Musical.ly, combine the apps, and take on YouTube the leading video platform.

Two months after TikTok was launched, they bought Musical.ly for $1 billion. It was a gamble at the time, but the best move to make.

It gave TikTok a quick start in the four-fifths of the world. Many companies would have kept the name Musical.ly, which was well-known at the time. ByteDance didn't. Long term, TikTok is a more unique, memorable, and distinctive name. Musical.ly was too generic and too specific. Names are challenging; they need to be narrow to get the brand off the ground, but they also need to be able to grow with the company.

By merging the brands and using a better name, TikTok could focus on one enemy: YouTube. A vital difference many don't mention when discussing TikTok's success is the vertical nature of the videos. Nobody shot or watched vertical videos before TikTok.

YouTube was the first online platform for Internet videos. When it was launched in 2005, you could only watch videos on computers screens, which are horizonal. Then the smartphone arrived, and YouTube went mobile. But when watching videos on a phone, you had to reorient the device horizontally, like a computer screen. That is what we all did.

A big part of what made TikTok different was the focus not just on short videos but vertical videos only. Since phones are used vertically, it makes watching TikTok videos way more convenient. The videos are not necessarily better this way, but they are much easier to watch on a phone. The enemy was horizontal content.

Today, the debate between TikTok versus YouTube is raging. The two major brands are firmly entrenched in short/vertical versus long/horizontal content. Who will be the king of Internet video? YouTube has tried to mimic TikTok with "Shorts." Unlikely to work. Better to focus on your longer-form horizontal video focus.

TikTok is the most popular app in the world with more than 773 million downloads in 2024.[22] As of February 2025, ByteDance is valued at $400 billion and has more than a billion active users.[23]

The iPhone of China: Xiaomi

A Chinese global cell phone brand has enormous potential. One of the top candidates is Xiaomi. It is known as the iPhone of China.

An Enemy Fuels Debate

Xiaomi was founded in 2010 by Chinese entrepreneur Lei Jun. It quickly became one of the world's leading smartphone brands. Like Steve Jobs, Lei Jun is famous for his captivating presentation style and focus on high-quality design. He spends a lot of time talking to the media to promote the brand. To make your brand famous, it helps to make your CEO famous too.

What built the Xiaomi brand was producing high-quality, well-designed phones at affordable prices. This propelled Xiaomi to success both in China and globally where it sells it phones.

Today Xiaomi is no longer just a cell phone brand. They have expanded into all sorts of categories such as headphones, monitors, speakers, smart lighting, fans, air purifiers, robot vacuums, cordless screwdrivers, photo printers, and air compressors. As if having the iPhone as the enemy wasn't hard enough to deal with, now they are competing against Dyson, DeWalt, Sonos, HP, Philips, Roomba, and more.

Next came a Xiaomi car. For years, the Internet was filled with speculation of an Apple iCar. It never came. Perhaps this fueled Lei Jun to do what Jobs never did. In March 2024, Xiaomi launched its first electric vehicle. The SU7, starting at just $30,000, offers Porsche-like looks with cutting-edge tech.

Of course, getting a new EV brand to market was much easier for Lei Jun than Jobs. China's electric car makers have been the beneficiaries of billions of dollars' worth of state support. And the supply chain is practically wrapped up inside the nation, including two of the world's largest battery makers.

So far customers have been wowed by the car's style, technology, and price. In December 2024, Xiaomi sold 25,815 SU7s compared with 21,046 for Tesla's Model 3.[24] Tesla sales have plunged more than 50 percent in China, where local brands not only are launching exciting new models but offer very steep discounts.

But to put these numbers in perspective: In China in February 2025 alone 720,000 EVs were sold. Of those, BYD, the world's largest EV builder, sold 322,846 units with 45 percent market share.[25]

The launch of Xiaomi's car has become the company's new focus, at least for its CEO. According to Daniel Desjarlais, the company's global spokesperson, Xiaomi has managed to push so aggressively and successfully into the EV market because Lei Jun has made it a priority. "Having him hands-on for the project has been part of the reason that we're doing so well," Desjarlais said. "He's the secret sauce."[26]

He is the secret sauce, no doubt, like Jensen Huang is at Nvidia. But one CEO and company chasing too many fast-moving categories is a recipe for disaster in the long term. Cars and cell phones are two incredibly fast and complicated categories. While making a few thousand cars is one thing, getting to mass production will be another. Meeting demand and delivery schedules is already a headache at Xiaomi.

Xiaomi should not forget smartphones. After all, it's their core business. Lei Jun is best not to neglect what he worked so hard to build. According to Canalys, Xiaomi's global smartphone shipments ranked among the top three smartphone brands globally for the seventeenth consecutive quarter, with a market share of 13.8 percent.[27] But as we know, market share can disappear in a heartbeat if you don't keep up with technology. Remember, Apple and Samsung aren't distracted by making cars.

The Tesla of China: XPeng

The world is waiting to see who the Elon Musk and Tesla of China will be. There has been a ton of press covering the potential brands and candidates. While America has two major electric brands in Tesla and Rivian, China is home to more than 300 electric vehicle brands. Time will tell which companies will survive and which can build a powerful global brand.

Founded in 1995, originally as a rechargeable battery maker, BYD has now become a dominant global manufacturer of electric vehicles. In 2024, BYD and Tesla were the world leaders, both producing about the same number of electric vehicles.

The problem is, what's a BYD? The letters did not even stand for anything until the marketing team recently made up the "Build Your Dreams" definition. Which doesn't make much sense as a name. What do you drive? A build your dreams. Huh? BYD is a weak brand,

An Enemy Fuels Debate

but a current sales leader. Time will tell if they can leverage the sales to build the brand.

Tesla started as a high-end brand and still carries the perception of premium in the mind. We are waiting for what the Tesla of China will be.

One candidate is XPeng. They recently hired us to help with their strategy. While it was founded in 2014, the brand first made waves in 2020 with the launch of the XPeng P7, the first car with level-three driving automation in China. The car could perform most driving tasks, but human override was still required.[28]

In 2023, the launch of the XPeng G6 was met with great fanfare. The model was instrumental in establishing the brand as a potential Tesla Model Y rival. Google it; you will find endless comparison stories, videos, and posts. "Is XPeng G6 a Model Y killer?" While they have not exactly killed the Model Y, they have gotten a lot of attention.

He Xiaopeng, the founder of XPeng, is an Elon Musk–type figure in China. A billionaire, innovator, and tech giant who makes the news a lot. While Musk has rockets and SpaceX; Xiaopeng has flying cars.

At the January 2024 CES tech trade show in Las Vegas, the company displayed a model of his flying car and said it would begin deliveries toward the end of 2025. While we are still waiting for the flying cars, the PR surrounding it has strengthened XPeng's image as a high-end brand using sophisticated technology.

As with Lei Jun and Xiaomi, Xiaopeng is the key component of XPeng's publicity strategy. He is becoming well known as a thought leader in EV technology. While the press is beneficial, the brand would benefit from a focus.

To succeed, Xiaopeng should focus on one idea to build the brand globally. For BMW it was "driving," for Volvo it was "safety," for Subaru it was "all-wheel drive."

According to *Forbes* magazine, "Analysts say XPeng has developed one of the best assisted driving products in China."[29] AI-assisted driving could be a powerful focus. As the pioneer and leader in autonomous driving in China, they can leverage this strength and focus globally. While the category is small now, self-driving cars are likely the future. Leaders need to think ahead like Jensen Huang did at Nvidia to position the brand to be ready to seize the day. To own the idea, they need to focus exclusively on it. Every XPeng needs to have AI-assistance features come standard. No XPeng should be a dumb car—they all need AI.

Now of course there are challenges. As a Chinese company, XPeng needs the same access to detailed data and maps in all countries as they do in China. And they will need to continue to heavily invest in research and development for AI and self-driving. But as my father famously told a banking client in the 1980s, "I gave you the idea; you figure out how to change the bank." The idea was to position United Jersey as the fast-moving bank which the client did and was a big success. The enemies were the big slow banks in New York City.

Core Concepts: An Enemy Fuels Debate

- Without a clear difference, there can be no debate.
- A debate gives people something specific to talk about and take a stand on.
- A debate leads to more detailed discussions allowing your brand story to shine.
- A debate engages, creates buzz and gives a sense of belonging to the brand tribe.

Chapter 8

Wielding a Visual Hammer

A visual hammer is a powerful tool to drive a positioning idea into the mind with emotion, memorability, and distinctiveness. In relation to your enemy, your visual difference is just as important as your strategic one. Once you establish a visual hammer, it visually reinforces your position and hammers your distinctiveness, authenticity, and leadership. Consider the blue box for Tiffany's, the Golden Arches for McDonald's, the red sole of a Louboutin, and the green jacket given to the winner of the Masters.

■ ■ ■

Positioning started as a verbal concept. You build a brand by owning a word in the mind. Your strategy, brand name, category name, focus, and slogan are all expressed in words. Companies, agencies, and consultants agonize over the selection of every word.

Yet the best way into a mind is not with words. The best way into a mind is with visuals. Words alone can never replace the emotional impact of a visual.

But not just any visual. You need a "visual hammer" that hammers a verbal nail. Think of these: Marlboro's cowboy. Coca-Cola's contour bottle. Corona's lime. Ferrari's prancing horse.

The cowboy hammers "masculinity." The contour bottle hammers "authenticity." The lime hammers "genuine Mexican beer." The prancing horse hammers "horsepower."

To be visualized, your verbal positioning idea needs to be specific, not broad. How would you visualize quality, great service, or innovation? You can't.

In fact, your verbal strategy may need to be adjusted to make it more visual, even if it means it becomes slightly less accurate. BMW is more accurately described as a performance car. But how do you visualize performance? You can't really. "The Ultimate Driving Machine" is a better verbal nail because it is more easily visualized by cars driving on winding roads. *Driving* is a visual word.

Trademarks vs. Visual Hammers

A trademark is not a visual hammer. Almost every brand has a trademark, but very few have a visual hammer. While a trademark can become well-known, unless it also communicates something, it isn't a visual hammer. Accenture has the > mark. Deloitte has a green dot. Ernst & Young has a yellow accent mark. Many people recognize these. But what meaning do they convey? Having a dot is better than nothing, I suppose. But having a visual hammer is the goal.

Names like Target, Domino's, Panda Express, JetBlue, Red Hat, Goldfish, Green Giant, LongHorn Steakhouse, and Shell all led to the creation of powerful visual hammers. That's why selecting a name that can be visualized is so valuable. How can you visualize a made-up word like Accenture?

One visual hammer Accenture did put to great use for six years was Tiger Woods. "We know what it takes to be a Tiger. High performance. Delivered." The campaign connected the traits Tiger used to win with the qualities needed in the business world, such as determination, strategy, and resilience. It was incredibly successful in building Accenture's brand in the mind. Tiger worked with many brands, but he was strongly connected with Accenture. The company was spending $50 million a year on advertising, and Tiger appeared in 83 percent of the company's ads. This was a much higher percentage than for any of his other major sponsors according to TNS Media Intelligence.[1]

The problems began in 2009 when Tiger drove into a tree, got caught cheating, got divorced, and even worse stopped winning golf tournaments. Accenture quickly dumped him too. You can't promote delivering high performance with a visual hammer that is now labeled a loser.

(Interestingly, Tiger has mostly restored his reputation, which became official when he won the 2019 Masters. That victory marked his 15th major win and his first major win since the 2008 U.S. Open. Everybody loves a redemption story.)

The Power and Benefits of Visuals

What are words anyway? They are useful devices created by people to communicate the reality of nature. In other words, we use words to describe the visual world around us. Yet printed words and aural sounds lack power even when they are trying to communicate the very same thing as a visual.

Visuals Are More Emotional

Compare reading the word "baby" with seeing the image of a baby. Or reading a book versus watching a movie. Quite often people will laugh out loud or cry when watching a movie; however, they are unlikely to show the same outward emotional response when reading the book version the movie was based on.

Words and slogans are important, but they lack the emotional impact of a visual. When your strategy and even your name is communicated visually, it is instantly more emotional.

Emotion is the glue that sticks a memory in your mind. Think about your past. What do you remember most? Most likely you remember the events with a high emotional connection, such as the day you met your partner, the birth of your child, 9/11, making your first speech, bombing on stage. And what specifically comes to mind for these events? Words or visuals? Memories are often referred to as pictures in our mind.

The events in your memory are almost always tied to a visual. Grab your phone and compare looking at your photo feed versus your calendar feed. Your photos likely trigger an emotional response. Our phone's photo album is a visual diary of our lives. Why are we constantly taking all these photos anyway? What we did, what our kids did, what we had for dinner, our pets, places we visited, the location of the car parked at the airport. To remember it, of course. My phone's calendar also keeps a record of the who, what, and where too. But it totally lacks emotion.

Visuals Are More Believable

Try this experiment. Take a photo of a beautiful woman and label it "Ugly Woman." Then ask people what they see. Despite the headline, most people will say they see a "beautiful woman" and comment somebody got the words wrong.

When a visual conflicts with the verbal, the visual always wins. The image is believed no matter what the words say. Seeing is believing. People are more trusting of what they see over the words they hear or read.

When you use a visual hammer, it makes your brand message more believable and credible. The best strategy combines both a verbal and visual together, and the reason you need both is because of what's inside your head.

In your head is a left brain and a right brain connected by the corpus callosum. The left brain excels in language and logical reasoning. The right brain excels in emotion and holistic thinking.

Visuals appeal to the intuitive and holistic right. Words appeal to the verbal and analytical left. The ultimate strategy hits both sides of the brain. The visual gets your attention; then sends the message to the left side of the brain to read or listen to the words.

Of course, lots of brands use visuals in marketing. However, when the visual isn't a hammer, it doesn't usually have much power. For example, how many times do you remember a commercial but totally forget what brand was being advertised? Happens a lot. The visual gets remembered, but unless it has a strong connection to the brand, it is useless.

Despite the attention to the power of the visual, most marketing programs lack them. The main reason is usually that the verbal idea they are trying to communicate is too broad. Unless you have a narrow focus, it is impossible to identify a visual to represent your idea in a dramatic way.

Visuals Are More Repeatable

Honestly, people don't want to read any more words than they have to. Reading is work. Visuals are practically effortless to process. As a result, visuals are more welcoming, appealing, and way less annoying.

Therefore, your visual hammer can and should be used as much as possible and on everything. Target's target visual is on everything. Think about it. If the bag had TARGET written all over it, it would be loud and annoying. But the Target visual is accepted and appreciated.

Same with Coca-Cola's contour bottle. Cola-Cola wisely uses the iconic bottle visual hammer on everything, including cups, cans, billboards, commercials, social media, delivery trucks, and more. And no need to worry about reality when it comes to a visual hammer. Not much Coke is sold in glass bottles and hasn't been for decades. But the use of the visual hammer on the cans of Coca-Cola transfers the authenticity of the original bottle into the product now sold in a can.

Consistency and repetition of your visual hammer will increase your authenticity and keep imitators at bay. Just about every watch maker has copied the unique watchband of Rolex, yet these products are all viewed as "fake Rolexes."

Naming Your Visual Hammer

After all the talk on how powerful visuals are, it is a good idea to use words to give your visual hammer a name. Naming your visual hammer emphasizes its uniqueness and establishes its existence. When you have a baby, you always give it a name. The same is true of a visual hammer. You need to give it a name so you and your consumers can talk about it. For example:

- Coca-Cola's "contour" bottle
- Nike's "Swoosh"
- Air Jordan's "Jumpman"
- Mercedes' "Tri-Star"
- McDonald's "Golden Arches"

A great visual hammer doesn't have to be created by a fancy firm. Nike famously paid Carolyn Davidson, a graphic design student at Portland State University, $35 for the design. As the pioneer and leader in athletic shoes, Nike just needed a simple visual that was easy to see on the shoes. Nike then wisely gave it a name, the Swoosh. The Swoosh has become an iconic visual hammer that communicates leadership.

Without leadership there is way less opportunity to create a visual hammer out of nothing the way Nike did. Look at Adidas, Under Armour, Reebok, or New Balance. They have logos, but they are just shapes with no meaning and little emotion. It takes decades of leadership to establish a visual hammer that doesn't also communicate an idea on its own.

Puma isn't the leader, but it does have a visual hammer that reinforces its name. So, if you are not the leader and pioneer, a name that instantly lends itself to a visual is a great way to stand out and be memorable in a crowded field.

A Visual Hammer Logo

Every brand has a logo. Few have one that is also a visual hammer. What makes a logo a visual hammer? It can't be just words; it needs to include an image. The image should be simple and communicate your position. When your brand name is one that can be visualized, it is even better.

Apple: The Apple

When you combine being the pioneer with a visual hammer that reinforces your name, you are doubly blessed. Apple is one of these companies.

Originally, Apple used a trademark with six colors. The rainbow of colors was attractive, but not as distinctive as the current white logo. A visual hammer in a singular color, especially one that is different from your enemy, is best. So, don't judge your logo on attractiveness; judge it on distinction and what message it is communicating.

Steve Jobs introduced the white logo in 1998 when he returned to Apple. The change was a visible signal to the world that he was back and ready to revitalize and refocus the company on his minimalist design philosophy.

Apple also used its white color as an effective visual hammer for its earbuds, first used for the iPod and now for the iPhone. Traditionally all wires were black. They were a necessary evil to power up or listen in. The idea was to make the wires disappear, and nothing disappears better than black. Apple did the opposite and made its wires white.

Are white wires better? Nope. They get dirty. Do white wires make the sound better? Nope. It is just a color that makes Apple's products different. This visible distinction allows others to see from afar you are using an iPhone and not an Android.

Apple is really a company, not a brand. The Apple company owns many powerful brands that are individually filed in different folders in the mind. Mac, iPhone, AirPods, AirTags, iPad, and iPod (may it rest in peace). The past decade they have added a few products with the Apple name, such as Apple Watch, Apple TV, and Apple Vision; it's interesting to note these have been some of their less successful brands.

Apple originally sold Apple computers. But in 1994, to establish a new category of graphical user interface computers, they called the new product a Macintosh. A new name for the new category and also a type of Apple. It was the first of many new brand names Apple used to expand into new categories. However, while each brand name is unique, they are all unified under the one Apple logo. Brilliant.

Android: The Robot

In 2005, Google purchased a small startup called Android. With the help of the new Android team members, Google spent three years developing an operating system for mobile devices. They didn't call it Google OS, something IBM would have done. Google used the Android name and told their design team to create a logo that included a robot.

Android OS launched in 2008 with its now familiar and well-established visual hammer, the green robot. Again, a singular color is more memorable and makes the robot more distinctive. A white robot would have been a bad idea.

Android OS is different from Apple's iOS because it is open-sourced while iOS is closed. Each has advantages. But being open offers flexibility and customization, and it is free. Today Android is the most popular mobile OS in the world by a large margin. As of 2025, Android was the leader with 72 percent market share. Apple's iOS is second with 28 percent market share.[2]

Like the software, Google decided to make the logo open-sourced too. "We decided it would be a collaborative logo that everybody in the world could customize," Google's designer said. "That was pretty daring."[3] Most companies, of course, defend their trademark from copycats, and million-dollar lawsuits have been filed over the rights to corporate insignia. This one would remain free. The Android logo has been dressed up as a ninja and even transformed into a limited-edition Kit-Kat bar.

Google has made some updates and refinements to the robot over the years. But this iconic visual hammer remains true to the green nerd in all of us.

Snapchat: The Ghost

Snapchat was founded in 2011 by Evan Spiegel, Reggie Brown, and Bobby Murphy, all students at Stanford University. Brown reportedly came up with the idea of a social media app that enabled users to post photos and videos that disappeared from the site after a few moments. It was first released as "Picaboo," but a few months later, Spiegel and Murphy forced Brown out and relaunched the brand as Snapchat. Snapchat is a better name with fewer syllables and allows their posts to be called *snaps*. However, the boo idea was strong because it communicates the brand's difference and became the inspiration for the visual hammer.

Identifying the enemy was essential to the brand's positioning. The enemy was Facebook and its sister brand Instagram. On Facebook and Instagram everybody was sharing the curated highlights of their lives and they all looked so perfect and exciting. We all started getting FOMO (fear of missing out) believing others were having fun while we were being left out. On top of that, what you may have posted years ago while drunk in college was now not only visible to your grandma but also potential job recruiters.

In the company's first-ever blog post, Spiegel made his case for Snapchat as a new way to share information that is intended to disappear. "After hearing hilarious stories about emergency detagging of Facebook photos before job interviews and Photoshopping blemishes out of candid shots before they hit the Internet (because your world would crumble if anyone found out you had a pimple on the 38th day of 9th grade), there had to be a better solution. Snapchat isn't about capturing the traditional Kodak moment. It's about communicating with the full range of human emotions—not just what appears to be pretty or perfect."[4]

In other words, younger users didn't want their social media history to come back to haunt them. Which is why the ghost visual hammer is perfect. They placed the white ghost on a bright yellow background, which makes the logo extra distinct.

Instacart: The Carrot

Instacart was founded in San Francisco in 2012 as a grocery delivery company. Today, they are the king of grocery deliveries in the United States with a 73 percent market share.[5] Customers order groceries through the Instacart app or website and then have their items delivered directly to their home by a personal shopper or pick them up at a designated store.

The brand's visual hammer is an orange carrot. Are carrots the only thing they deliver? Of course not. But showing a basket of food is less memorable. Better to pick one specific item to represent them all. The carrot is great. It communicates fresh, fun, and affordable.

Who is the enemy? The other big dogs in food delivery: DoorDash and Uber Eats. DoorDash is focused on restaurant delivery. Uber Eats is a line-extension of Uber's ride business. The carrot clearly differentiates Instacart as the app that delivers groceries. Nobody orders raw carrots from takeout.

However, all three companies have started to blur the lines. DoorDash's 2025 Super Bowl ad featured comedian Nate Bargatze ordering groceries, dog toys, and disco balls from DoorDash. Are you kidding me? Advertising should be used to reinforce your strength, not expand your position. DoorDash is dominant in restaurant delivery; they should have reminded us of that.

In 2022, Instacart cut most of the carrot off the logo. It is now a green arrow with a little orange top. Why? According to the company's blog, "Over the years, we have evolved to be grocery-first but not grocery only."[6] They want to expand to home goods, beauty, pharmacy, and office supplies, and they are afraid of looking like they only deliver groceries. A visual hammer should represent and reinforce your focus. It is a visual symbol of your leadership. Cutting the carrot cuts down that value. TikTok didn't get rid of the music note after expanding to include all types of videos. While Instacart's app tile has the whole carrot, the logo and marketing no longer does.

The whole carrot is much better for introducing the brand to new customers. Grocery delivery is the carrot that gets you hooked on the app. Keeping it would have been unlikely to deter people from using the app to order stuff from Walgreens or Sephora too. Once they are on the app you can promote that. A whole carrot is better than just the top.

Changing Your Visual Hammer Can Be Dangerous

If your brand is more than 100 years old, there have likely been some changes made to the logo over the years. Pepsi is one of these. The initial unreadable script used in 1898 was thankfully changed several times. However, by the 1960s they had locked in on a simple and memorable visual identity. Pepsi with a swirl of red and blue. Then in 1991, they began to make changes.

In the 1990s they wanted to upgrade the logo for the digital age, and in the 2000s they refreshed it for the millennium. But it was the 2008 redesign that did the most damage and created the most debate. Pepsi's new logo was unrecognizable from what it had been before.

The redesign was controversial to say the least, with mixed reactions from both consumers and critics. A few praised the modern and minimalistic approach, while others felt it strayed too far from the brand's established identity. The design brief was leaked on Reddit and offered an eyebrow-raising glimpse into the rebranding fiasco. The brief pontificated over magnetic fields, the theory of relativity, and the gravitational pull of Pepsi.[7] Most felt it pretentious for a can of soda.

In 2023, they straightened things out by essentially going back to the Pepsi logo from the 1960s with a few very minor tweaks.

The lesson in all this is once you have an iconic logo and visual hammer established, don't mess with it. Two other brands that did the same thing are Pizza Hut and Burger King. Both have now reverted like Pepsi to their original, classic designs.

There are times when the simplification of a logo is a good idea. Mercedes-Benz, for example, greatly simplified its Tri-Star visual hammer in 2008. The simple design was easier to see on the cars.

But tread carefully when it comes to changes. When simplifying, you need to be careful not to go overboard or you risk losing what the logo used to clearly visualize and stand for.

Honestly, I prefer Instagram's original logo that communicates instant photos. While perhaps it needed some simplification, I think they went overboard. They simplified it to the point that it is no longer recognizable to the next generation as an instant camera. That's a bummer.

A Singular Visual Hammer Color

A singular color is a great way to create a visual hammer. It is also a good way to differentiate your brand from your enemy. Too often colors are judged by what they communicate. Blue is corporate. Red is attention. Green is the environment. Purple is royal. Yellow is caution. But if your enemy is blue, your top priority is to be anything but blue.

The reality is few companies focus on one color. But they should. It's not about looking pretty; it is about standing out from the crowd.

Tiffany and Blue

Tiffany's was founded in 1837 in Lower Manhattan. Charles Tiffany first started using the now trademarked Tiffany Blue color (Pantone 1837) in 1845 on the cover of his Blue Book, a mail order catalog for his stationery. In 1853, he changed the store to focus on fine jewelry.

The turning point for the brand came 30 years later when Tiffany's pioneered a new category. In 1886, Tiffany's launched a new style of diamond engagement ring featuring a raised claw with six-progs to hold a diamond securely but visibly atop a ring band. This exposed more of the diamond and, with it, made it more sparkling. It was the opposite of how other rings were set. "All diamonds were set in a bezel so only the crown (top) was visible," says Russell Shor, senior analyst for the Gemological Institute of America.[8]

This new ring came nestled inside the first signature blue Tiffany box. The combination of being first in a new category and using the blue box visual hammer made Tiffany famous. While the box became every bit as coveted as the ring, the ring is what made the box powerful.

By 1905, Tiffany was hailed as America's leading purveyor of fine jewelry. Stories about the "Diamond King" Charles Tiffany and the box made the news. In 1906, the *New York Sun* reported that Charles Tiffany "has one thing in stock that you cannot buy of him for as much money as you may offer; he will only give it to you. And that is one of his boxes."[9]

In 1961, Tiffany's allowed Paramount Pictures to film part of *Breakfast at Tiffany's* inside their flagship location. To prevent the theft of any blue boxes, 40 armed guards were posted around the store.[10] While maybe 10 guards would have been necessary, using 40 armed guards was great PR, as was the movie.

The box is the visual hammer, and today Tiffany's sells a whole lot more than jewelry, but everything they sell comes in the signature blue box. It unites the brand under one visual hammer.

Louboutin Shoes and Red

When it comes to footwear, there is nothing more iconic than Christian Louboutin's red sole. There are lots of expensive shoe brands, but only one comes with red soles. Like Tiffany's blue box and iPod's white wires, the red soles do nothing to make the shoes better; they only serve to make them distinctive and recognizable as "Loubis."

The red soles' origin story is the stuff of fashion folklore. In 1993, two years after launching his independent business, Louboutin designed a shoe collection inspired by Andy Warhol's *Flowers* lithograph. The prototype came back, but the design didn't "pop" like Louboutin had hoped. After seeing his assistant painting her nails, the designer had an "aha" moment and took red nail polish and painted the soles red.

Louboutin's focus is on high heels, the stiletto. In an interview with *British Vogue* in 2012, Louboutin said: "People say I am the king of painful shoes. I don't want to create painful shoes, but it is not my job to create something comfortable. I try to make high heels as comfortable as they can be, but my priority is design, beauty, and sexiness. I'm not against them, but comfort is not my focus."[11]

Exactly. Louboutin has focused on one thing for more than 30 years. That is what makes it such a success. While Louboutin has created countless shoe collections, one thing is always the same on every pair: the soles are red.

Crumbl Cookies and Pink

Crumbl combined heavy amounts of sugar and social media to create the perfect five-dollar, 700-calorie, Instagrammable cookie served in a pink box. Every Sunday at 8 p.m. Eastern, fans across the country check Crumbl Cookies' social media to discover the week's newest flavors. Weekly menu changes are a key ingredient of the brand; they generate excitement as well as FOMO. Just watching the social media feed for its cookies is an indulgent pleasure.

The fast-growing chain now has more than 1,000 Crumbl cookie shops in the United States and Canada. Franchisees are generating more than $1 billion in annual sales.

The pink box doesn't make the cookie taste any better, but it has been a cornerstone of the brand since the beginning. "I felt like once we found the box, it really elevated the brand, and it gave us a sense of direction and the box really is the brand," co-founder Sawyer Hemsley recalled.[12]

"How could something as simple as a box really make that big of a difference, from who you are to how you differentiate?" said co-founder Jason McGowan.[13] Because it's not just a box; it's a visual hammer.

The brand stands for weekly rotating cookie flavors, the distinctive pink box now represents this idea in the mind as a visual hammer.

That begs the question, what should Mrs. Fields, the "Original Gangster" of cookie shops, do? No mall trip in the 1980s was complete without eating a freshly baked Mrs. Fields' chocolate chip cookie. Back in the day Debbie Fields was an incredible spokesperson for the brand. Her story of being a chocolate lover, starting a cookie shop, and growing the company was legendary. But she isn't part of the company anymore.

First, what they shouldn't do. Mrs. Fields's should not launch a bunch of crazy cookie flavors. You can't out Crumbl, Crumbl. Instead, they should do the opposite, promote their iconic chocolate chip cookie that only uses the best chocolate. You want pink frosting? We don't serve that at Mrs. Fields.

The arrival of Crumbl has brought attention back to the cookie category. It is the perfect time for Mrs. Fields to strike back as the alternative to the pink sticky sweetness of Crumbl. Tell Debbie's amazing story of chocolate and entrepreneurship to a new generation of women. Remember, Crumbl is owned by two dudes.

A Visual Hammer Package

A visual hammer package involves using a new approach to packaging a familiar product. The product being essentially the same; only the packaging is different. The enemy is the product packaged another way.

Over time the optimal packaging for any given category is achieved. Today, all toothpaste comes in tubes and all tissues in pop-up boxes. But the leading brands in both these categories first established themselves with a unique packaging idea. That idea helped solidify them as leaders and innovators in their categories.

Before Kleenex pop-up tissue boxes, bundles of tissues were often sold in bulk without a box. Before Colgate toothpaste tubes, the paste was in jars, and you scooped it out with a little spoon.

If you don't remember this, I don't either. If a new packaging idea is your visual hammer, it won't usually last forever. Competitors will copy the format, and the excitement of the innovation will fade. At this point your brand name needs to be the differentiator and recognized as the pioneer. Even though all the packages look the same, I seek the one that says Kleenex because it's the real thing.

Graza: Olive Oil in a Squeeze Bottle

Chefs and home cooks have been using plastic squeeze bottles for oil for 50 years; putting olive oil in a bottle was not revolutionary. But branding it and selling it this way to consumers was.

Andrew Benin was living in Spain with his in-laws while between jobs. He spent time exploring the local sights driving from Cordoba to Jaen. After enjoying the best home-cooked meals he had ever eaten and viewing olive trees for miles, Andrew was inspired.

"On that trip, I felt like I tasted olive oil for the first time...My family in Spain thought I had totally lost my mind, speaking about olive oil 24/7, but my wheels were cranking," Benin recounted on his company's blog.[14]

Back in New York City, Benin sat down with Gramercy Tavern Executive Chef Mike Anthony with the intention of impressing him with all the crazy good oils he discovered in Spain. Instead, Mike quickly put him in his place. "He made it clear that the world didn't need another purveyor of small batch, super fancy, super expensive olive oil from Europe," Benin wrote.[15] He was right. More of the same wasn't how to disrupt the industry. Plenty of new brands took the high-end purveyor approach with fancy names, bottles, and prices.

Graza did the opposite. The brand focus is on accessibility and fun from the package to the pricing to the branding. The oil is well regarded, but the plastic bottle is the star. Graza's recognizable, easily maneuverable squeeze bottles allow novice cooks to mimic how a pro uses oil in a restaurant kitchen. The brand vibe is friendly and unfussy. Graza is for every day, not just special meals.

Graza goes out of its way to make the product approachable by explaining the basics in a friendly way. There are two oils, and the names make it unmistakably clear which one is better suited for what. Graza "Sizzle" is extra virgin cooking oil. Graza "Drizzle" is extra virgin finishing oil.

Most of us bought EVOO because Rachael Ray told us to, never understanding why it was better or what it even was. Graza breaks it down into simple-to-understand terms. Making home chefs like me feel like the Bear.

Founded in 2022, Graza did well right out of the gate. Benin's experience in both fancy restaurants and direct-to-consumer startups such as Warby Parker, Casper, Oura Ring, and Magic Spoon positioned him well to raise money as well as get the brand in the hands of influencers, especially the online chefs teaching a new generation to cook on TikTok and Instagram. Within a few months it was on the shelves of Whole Foods. Today, they are in Target, and even Walmart. The plastic bottle is already being copied by other brands, but the brand name Graza and its green bottle visual hammer will continue to set it apart as the brand that is the original.

Black Box: Wine in a Box

Boxed wine had been around for decades, but it was relegated to the lowest level of the quality pyramid and the store shelf. Sold at bargain basement prices in basic packaging, wine in a box was offered in white or red. While Graza used packaging that top chefs were using, creating a premium brand of wine in a box would be a more difficult sell. Changing the perception that good wine only comes in bottles would take the right brand and great marketing. The brand to do it was Black Box.

Black Box was the first premium box wine. It was launched in 2003 by Constellation Brands, which also owns the Robert Mondavi winery. But it wasn't their idea. Some executives happened to taste the brand during a sampling. They were so impressed, they purchased the brand from the young entrepreneur who invented it.

The black box looks premium, sleek, and sophisticated. But getting people to try it would take more effort than just having an upscale box, even if it was a visual hammer.

Usually when big companies buy small brands, they muck them up. Constellation was determined not to do that. "We added some marketing muscle to it, but everything else remained the same," said Chris Fehrnstrom, CMO of Constellation.[16]

To overcome the negative perception problem of the box, they did three things. First, they embarked on an extensive sampling program. Here is where a big company with deep pockets and retail connections is super helpful. If tasting the wine got Mondavi executives excited about the product, all they needed to do was to have consumers try it too. But if consumers saw the wine come out of a box, their mind would reject it as not tasting good. So, they used a little trickery in the sampling.

"We used to decant the wine when we invited consumers to sample it," Fehrnstrom said, "and only after people tasted it and were impressed, we brought out the Black Box. A bit of Candid Camera surprise ensued."

That was only step one. Enjoying a free sample is one thing, but putting a big black box in your cart is another. Consumers needed the brand to gain recognition so they could feel comfortable and confident if anybody saw them buying it. For this they needed credentials, and in wine there are no better credentials than medals. They aggressively entered the wine in contests. Ten years after launching, Black Box had racked up 40 Gold Medals and was the recipient of 27 *Wine Enthusiast* magazine Best Buys.

Since everybody doesn't necessarily read *Wine Enthusiast*, they noted all the awards on the box itself. Another signal of premium wine is being appellation-specific and using vintage dates, so they added that too. With a big black box, there was plenty of room to tell the brand story and show off the medals.

The last element was selling the convenience. Very importantly, this didn't come first. Or even second. Only after the wine brand was loved and had credentials would this work. A 3-liter box of Black Box is the equivalent of four bottles of wine. The box offers a compelling price point when you add it up. When comparing similar wines in a bottle, Black Box is 40 percent cheaper. On top of this, with its re-closable twist-off cap, the wine lasts from four to six weeks. Never feel bad about throwing out old wine you didn't finish the night or two before. While these are very real and persuasive reasons, they are best used by consumers who use the brand to justify buying the brand. It makes them feel smart. And gives them a story to tell their friends.

Today, the brand is owned by E. & J. Gallo. Black Box remains the leader in the premium box wine category, a category that has been one of the fastest growing in the industry for years. The website reminds visitors that Black Box is the most awarded boxed wine.[17] They have continued to rack up awards and have more than 100 gold medals and over 30 Best Buy awards.[18] And these distinctions are still front and center on the box—well, a little to the right side, but you know what I mean.

A Visual Hammer for You

Want to stand out and build your own brand? First find a focus, and then add a visual hammer. Clothing, glasses, sunglasses, flowers, color. Finding your signature look and sticking to the uniform is the way to be noticed and remembered.

Steve Jobs, Founder, Apple: A Black Turtleneck

The black turtleneck was Steve's uniform and visual hammer. It represented his ethos, genius, and focus. For Jobs it wasn't done to build his brand; he wanted to reduce the number of decisions he had to make in the mornings so he could focus on his work. But it certainly did visualize his brand and increased his visibility.

As Ryan Tate wrote in Gawker, the turtleneck "helped make him the world's most recognizable CEO."[19]

It is interesting to note that Elizabeth Holmes of Theranos adopted the black turtleneck to try to convince the world of her own Jobs-like brilliance. Being a copycat won't work. You can't just wear Steve's black turtleneck and expect people to think you are an innovator. It is the reverse. Your success will make your signature style stand for something: you.

Jensen Huang, Founder/CEO, NVIDIA: A Black Leather Jacket

Tech's current king, NVIDIA CEO Jensen Huang, long ago chose a black leather jacket as his signature look. He's worn leather jackets for more than 20 years and has several. Mr. Huang wore a black leather jacket when he was on the cover of *Time* as one of its people of the year in 2021.

He also wears the jacket no matter what. According to one observer, when the NVIDIA chief was walking around Computex in Taipei in his leather jacket, he was asked how he could stand the heat. (The temperature on the day of his keynote was between 79 and 90 degrees.)

"I'm always cool," Mr. Huang responded.[20] Great answer.

Bill McDermott, Chairman/CEO, ServiceNow: *Sunglasses*

The accident that cost Bill McDermott his eye led to his signature sunglass look. In 2015, McDermott slipped on the stairs at his brother's home during the night while holding a glass of water. The glass shattered, a shard punctured his eye, and he briefly lost consciousness. He was in surgery for over nine hours that night and has had more than 10 operations in total. But it hasn't slowed him down; it made him stronger.

"I am living proof that vision is not just what you see. My accident has given me so much strength, so much resolve, so much passion," McDermott told CNBC in an interview.[21]

At the time he was CEO of SAP and was back at work within two months. He continued to serve as the CEO of SAP until October 2019, and by November that year, he was appointed as the CEO of ServiceNow. He is one of the most recognizable tech titans in the industry.

John Fetterman, US Senator, Pennsylvania: *A Hoodie and Gym Shorts*

While Donald Trump's 2025 presidential inauguration was moved inside due to the bitter cold outside, Sen. John Fetterman didn't let the cold bother him. Fetterman arrived at the US Capitol in his usual outfit: a pair of gray shorts, a black-hooded sweatshirt, and black sneakers.

The congressional rules of attire were relaxed in 2023, which allows Fetterman to wear a more casual outfit.

"Aren't there more important things we should be talking about rather than if I dress like a slob?" Fetterman said in an interview on MSNBC.[22]

Slob or not, Fetterman has made the news for many reasons. His uniform is the opposite of every other senator's buttoned-up look. It sends a message; he is a regular guy who got elected and isn't planning to conform to the rules of Washington, DC.

Shirley Franklin, Mayor of Atlanta: A Large Flower

Shirley Franklin was known for wearing a signature flower. She served as the city's mayor from 2002 to 2010 and was notable for being the first African American woman to lead a major Southern city in the United States. She always wore a large flower pinned to her lapel during public appearances and interviews.

Anna Wintour, Editor-in-Chief, Vogue: A Chic Bob with Bangs and Black Sunglasses

Anna Wintour has been Editor-in-Chief of *Vogue* for 34 years. She is one of the most powerful women in the fashion industry and the driving force behind the Met Gala.

In the world of fashion where trends are constantly changing and as the leader of the most influential magazine that covers these fashion trends, Anna did the opposite. One look, one style. She has never wavered from her signature aesthetic, proving that true style isn't about following trends; it's about defining your own.

Laura Ries, Author: Red

Practicing what you preach isn't easy. But positioning is in my blood. Years ago, I picked red as my color. Red outfits on stage and for media interviews. Red logo. Red positioning heads. And I still drive my dad's red Corvette convertible.

Core Concepts: Wielding a Visual Hammer

- Words alone can never replace the emotional power of a visual.
- A visual hammer visualizes your positioning idea.
- A visual hammer is distinctive, memorable, and repeatable.
- A visual hammer reinforces a brand's authenticity and leadership.

Chapter 9

Nvidia: A Positioning Success Story

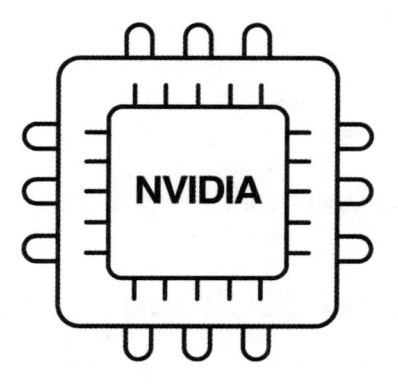

A review of Nvidia's historic rise to success is the perfect way to understand and appreciate the power of positioning, focus, saying no, and the enemy. Most often we focus on what successful companies are doing today. And today everybody is watching Nvidia's every move. While that is interesting, as far as marketing goes, it is more important to study what they did to achieve their leadership. The hardest part of building a company is getting off the runway. Once you have become the most important AI computing company in the world, things get a little easier.

■ ■ ■

Nvidia has become one of the most valuable companies in the world. Jensen Huang, the CEO of Nvidia, was selected one of *Time Magazine* 100 most influential people. In *Time*'s 2024 article on why he is so influential, Mark Zuckerberg wrote, "I always admired leaders who have the grit and determination to stick with their vision for long periods of time. Jensen Huang is the clear leader of the tech industry in this regard."[1]

Huang has captained the Nvidia ship with grit and determination for more than 30 years. The credit for the company's success is not his alone. But the credit for overseeing the company's focus is certainly his.

The story of Nvidia is one every entrepreneur should study. It is a classic case of using all the theories we preach about, from positioning to focus to new categories to identifying the strategic enemy. Like many companies, Nvidia was not an instant success and faced many challenges and enemies along the way. Huang's incredible leadership and unrelenting focus led the way for Nvidia to achieve global dominance.

The Initial Focus: 3D Graphic Chips for PCs

Jensen Huang co-founded Nvidia along with Curtis Priem and Chris Malachowsky in 1993 in a booth of a Denny's restaurant. The three founders had a simple idea: to launch the first consumer 3D graphics chip company.[2]

The personal computer had evolved from its first inception in the 1980s. After Apple introduced the Macintosh in 1984 with its graphical user interface (GUI), it changed how people worked on PCs. It began to go from a text-oriented way to a graphically oriented way using icons and windows. And visual tasks became more important, from photo editing to desktop publishing to gaming and videos.

The release of Windows 3.0 in 1990 marked a significant turning point in bringing the graphical interface to all PCs. This excited Huang, Priem, and Malachowsky. They saw personal computers could one day be used by anybody for games with advanced graphics, but PCs would need better chips. They envisioned a future where the advanced simulator games they currently had to play on workstations could be made available to anybody with a PC and at a reasonable price.

Priem and Malachowsky came from Sun Microsystems and had worked on its GX graphics chips for six years. Sun workstations always had an advanced graphical interface. Windows was moving in this direction, but there wasn't a company focused on chips for the intense graphics processing that gaming required. They figured their workstation expertise could be leveraged to develop similar high-performance graphics cards for the growing PC/Windows market.

The First No

Before they even had a name for their new company, they were offered an incredible deal. Sun offered to license its entire portfolio of patents to their startup, including Priem's and Malachowsky's GX graphics chip designs. In exchange, they would agree to make their new chips compatible to run on workstations and personal computers.

A deal with Sun would have given them a large brand-name customer right off the bat and protect them from any possible copyright infringement claims from their former employer. Many entrepreneurs would have said yes without hesitation.

They said no. The problem was that if they did the deal, they would not have a focus. It would mean spending less time and resources on the PC market, which was where they felt the real opportunity lay.

The Name

The initial name they came up for their new chip was "GX Next Version" or "GXNV." But that name sounded like a GX copycat. They needed a new name to break from the past. Huang suggested they drop the GX and call their chip the NV1.

Now they needed a company name. One early idea was Primal Graphics. It sounded cool and used letters of two of the founders, PRI and MAL. But Huang was the leader; the name would need to include him too, but the possibilities using all three didn't sound great, such as Huaprimal, Prihuamal, and Malhuapri.

Connecting the name of the first product, NV1, with the company name was a better approach. It kept things unified for launch and kept it simple for getting into the mind.

They named the company NVision until they learned the name was already taken by a manufacturer of toilet paper. Huang suggested Nvidia, riffing on the Latin word *invidia*, meaning envy. Priem liked it and reminded them that they all hoped to make competitors "green with envy" one day.[3] On April 5, 1993, Nvidia was born.

The Second No

With the name for the company and the product secured, now they needed funding. Their meeting with the venture capital firm Kleiner Perkins, whose home-run investments included America Online and Sun Microsystems, was going well. The partners loved the graphics chip idea but insisted Nvidia needed to manufacture the chips too. After all, that is what Intel did.

Nvidia's intent was to focus only on designing chips. They had no special expertise in manufacturing, so why would they expand their focus and try to do that too? The answer to Kleiner was "We'll stick to what we are good at, and if that's not for you, it's not for you."

Their goal was to take over the PC graphics market; to do so, they needed to concentrate their resources on their single best opportunity instead of chasing multiple ones. Another no for the sake of maintaining focus. Same as they did when saying no to making chips that were compatible with Sun workstations.

At Sequoia Capital, the ask of the partners was different. Sequoia wanted them to define their focus even more clearly. "What are you?" asked Valentine, one of the partners. "Are you a gaming-console company? Are you a graphics company? Are you an audio company? You have to be one."

Priem answered back, "We're all of them!" and went into a deeply technical explanation only an engineer could understand. Valentine fired back. "Pick one; otherwise, you're going to fail because you don't know who you are."[4]

Against Valentine's advice, Sequoia gave Nvidia $1 million in funding.

There was a nugget of truth to Priem's answer. The future of Nvidia would eventually lead to chips that accelerated not just graphics but other computer functions such as AI. But they would need to be successful in graphics first.

The NV1 Mistake: Multimedia Instead of Graphics Only

Engineers love to innovate. Maintaining focus isn't easy when brilliant engineers have lots of creative ideas. Despite being told to focus on one idea by Sequoia, the founders went ahead and designed a multimedia chip that improved both the graphics and audio for computer games.

It was a mistake. Sales were dismal. They innovated to innovate without considering the market, the mind, or how the product could be positioned. Nvidia ended up competing against graphics, audio, and peripheral companies.

While NV1's graphics performance got attention, the addition of the sound was a problem. Nvidia's marketing director recalls being told several times by potential buyers, "We really like your graphics technology, so if you guys ever want to get rid of the audio, come back and see us."[5]

Chief engineer Scott Sellers of competitor 3dfx's Voodoo Graphics summed up Nvidia's NV1 mistake. "It wasn't the best graphics. It wasn't the best audio. It wasn't the best of anything."[6]

Huang learned a valuable lesson on the power of focus. "We were diluted across too many different areas. We learned it was better to do fewer things well than to do too many things, even though it looked good on a PowerPoint slide," he reflected.[7]

The hole in the mind was for a specialized chip that delivered the fastest graphics performance for PC games. Nvidia failed to focus and position the brand to fill that hole.

In a 2023 talk for the Berkley Haas Dean's Series, Huang shared how *Positioning: The Battle for Your Mind* taught him a lot and that it was one of his favorite books. He read it in his 30s, after one of Nvidia's board members, Harvey Jones, asked him a simple

Nvidia: A Positioning Success Story

question that at the time was impossible for him to answer: "How would you position this?" Not the features and benefits, but where in the mind, in the context of the ecosystem and competition, would you position it? A simple question that is the key to successful brand building.

During the talk, Huang gave some advice to the young students. "The sooner you realize the question [How will you position this?] exists, the better off you are going to be. Whatever idea you want to start, partly is what does it do, but partly is how are you going to position it. So if you start answering the question today, that's great."[8]

The NV1 mistake was trying to do too many things, instead of just one. When you focus, positioning is more easily accomplished. In the future, Nvidia would remember to answer both questions: What one thing does it do? And how will we position it?

Enemy #1: 3dfx's Voodoo Graphics

When 3dfx launched its Voodoo Graphics cards in October 1996, it didn't make the mistake the NV1 did. Voodoo positioned itself as the chip that could bring Silicon Graphics–level performance to personal computers at a fraction of the cost. Silicon Graphics (SGI) is known for producing the best high-end graphics used for computer-generated movie effects, including the dinosaurs in Steven Spielberg's *Jurassic Park*.

Voodoo's message was clear and specific: outsized graphics performance at a great price. Ross Smith, 3Dfx co-founder explained, "Last year at Comdex, Bill Gates played the Valley of Ra in our booth on a quarter-of-a-million-dollar SGI Reality Engine–based Voodoo Graphics simulator. That same real-time 3D graphics performance is now available to PC consumers for $299. That's righteous!"[9]

One game made Voodoo a success: Quake, the hottest first-person shooter game. It was the killer app that motivated consumers to upgrade their hardware. Sales of Voodoo went crazy.

3dfx was so successful at this time that they could have bought Nvidia but passed. They assumed Nvidia's bankruptcy was inevitable

152 *The Strategic Enemy*

and would pick up its talent and assets on the cheap later. Sadly, it was 3dfx that would go bankrupt in 2000 after acquiring STB Systems and attempting to expand into both manufacturing and distribution of chips. They should have stayed focused.

Fighting the Enemy at the Speed of Light

In 1996 Nvidia was on the ropes. They had laid off more than half the people at the company. To survive, Huang decided they needed to focus on developing the fastest graphics chip possible, and then beat the competition to market.

To make the chip faster, they used a 128-bit memory bus that could generate pixels at record-breaking speeds. It was also the largest chip ever designed and loaded with as many transistors as possible to boost performance. They named the chip the RIVA 128 for Real-time Interactive Video and Animation Accelerator.

Huang encouraged his employees to aim for achieving the "Speed of Light" in projects. Tasking them to find the fastest way possible, unconstrained by how it was done before or internal politics. The speed of light means getting to the market first. When you combine being first with the right product and positioning, it establishes your brand in the mind. Nvidia needed to make the speed of light happen for the RIVA 128.

Standard chip development usually takes two years. Nvidia didn't have the time or money for that. To speed things up, they did things differently. They developed the driver software before the prototype chip was completed. Then Huang pushed to spend $1 million on an emulator to drastically speed up testing time. It was a gamble; the million bucks cut the payroll runway down significantly.

When the RIVA 128 hit stores, Nvidia was nearly out of cash. The phrase "Our company is thirty days from going out of business" remains an unofficial corporate motto.[10] It reminds them to stay lean, mean, and focused.

At the 1997 Computer Game Developers Conference, Nvidia unveiled the RIVA 128. It instantly created buzz. The chips' performance was incredible. The RIVA 128 was not only able to outperform

3dfx's best cards but was also the fastest consumer graphics card ever. *PC Magazine* named the RIVA 128 an Editors' Choice product, and *PC Computing* named it Product of the Year for 1997.[11]

Nvidia finally delivered the right product at the right time.

Enemy #2: Intel

Soon after the successful launch of the RIVA 128, Intel announced its own graphics chip, the i740. It was a direct challenge to Nvidia. Intel was a feared enemy. They dominated the CPU chips, and now they were gunning for graphics chips. To stand out, Intel's chip had an eight-megabyte frame buffer and Nvidia's only had a four-megabyte one. Like most consumers, I'm not exactly sure how a frame buffer works either, but again like most consumers, basic math tells me eight is more than four.

With these numbers, Intel would cream Nvidia 8 to 4. Huang fired up his team. At an all-company meeting Huang proclaimed, "Intel is out to get us…Our job is to kill them before they put us out of business. We need to kill Intel."[12]

Nvidia knew they could not compete with a four-megabyte frame buffer. Luckily, they found the answer when Malachowsky realized they had left some spare capacity in the chip's silicon. They were able to rework the chip so it would have the same eight-megabyte frame buffer as Intel. The RIVA 128ZX offered better performance than the i740 and an eight-megabyte frame buffer. The mind processes these decisions in a simple way. Eight always sounds better than four. Unless you are playing golf.

A New Category and Focus: The GPU

By 1999, Nvidia was competing with 70 other graphics chip companies. Most often, companies competed on price when selling to manufacturers. To succeed and build the brand in the mind of consumers, Nvidia decided to do things differently.

While most chips were getting smaller and cheaper, Nvidia did the opposite. They built a larger card called GeForce 256 with more capabilities. While the other graphics cards cost $12–15, Nvidia's card would be $40–50.

The problem was that the technology, which included more pipelines and an engine for scaling 3D objects, was way too technical to communicate. What GeForce 256 needed was a simple way to position it in the mind of the consumer.

Nvidia's head of marketing, Dan Vivoli, an avid follower of positioning, came up with the strategy for GeForce. Vivoli suggested calling GeForce the first GPU, or graphics processing unit. "We invented a new category and instantly became the leader of it," Vivoli said.

When creating a new category, it is best to relate it to an existing one. The term GPU was easily understood. The GPU would be to graphics processing what the computers' CPU was to central processing. The CPU at the time was the most important and expensive chip in a computer; the new GPU category set it up to make it as important as the CPU.

The differences were easy to explain to just about anybody. A CPU processes each task one at a time; a GPU breaks complex tasks apart into small calculations and then processes them all at once. The CPU does linear computing; the GPU does parallel. Advanced graphics are best handled by parallel computing.

Except there was one problem: Nvidia's engineers questioned the GPU distinction by saying it wasn't technically accurate yet since the chip wasn't fully programmable. Luckily, the marketing team won out. The press release declared GeForce 256 as the world's first GPU. And shortly after, the chips were fully programmable.

The GeForce line was a huge hit. Its popularity was driven by the Quake video-game series, which used parallel computing to render monsters that players could shoot with a grenade launcher. Gamers looking for an edge upgraded their GeForce cards every time a new one came out.

What makes a category? Followers. Nvidia wisely never trademarked GPU; they wanted other companies to use the name of the category they pioneered. When the media and Intel started using the term GPU, they knew the category folder was firmly established in the mind.

Nvidia: A Positioning Success Story

Nvidia and Public Relations

Nvidia didn't have an outsized marketing budget, but they did have a focus and used public relations to build the brand.

When anybody bought a computer, they first consulted with their trusted "tech" friend or family member for advice on what to buy. But how did these so-called tech experts get their information? The media. They were likely avid readers of the half-dozen tech enthusiast websites and magazines such as *Tom's Hardware* and *PC Magazine*.

Dan Vivoli led an all-out effort to get to know and win over these tech writers, especially Thomas Pabst of *Tom's Hardware* and Nick Stam of *PC Magazine*.

They started holding Editors' Days. "We invited tech influencers to the factory and promised them they would not talk to any marketing people; they would only talk to engineers. We shared things we were working on to get feedback, since they were the experts and could provide insights into what consumers wanted. Plus, we figured if they helped us shape the chips, they might feel some ownership when they came out," recalled Vivoli.

Positive reviews and winning benchmarks are critical to establishing credibility. To make sure Nvidia's chips performed well, Vivoli built several Virtual Review labs. They studied exactly how *Tom's Hardware* or *PC Magazine* reviewed and benchmarked chips and then created a virtual "Tom" and "Nick" that would test the chips. Vivoli told his team to get in their heads and to write up a mock review as if it was written by them. In essence, Nvidia did their own review simulations of all new drivers and chips. If a chip failed these reviews, changes could be made. Later, they expanded from half a dozen virtual reviewers and virtualized as many media outlets as possible.

Apart from asking friends what computer to buy, gamers were influenced by the games themselves. Bill Rehbock, director of developer relations, created a program called "The way it's meant to be played." Nvidia invested heavily in technical support for game developers. The idea was to encourage developers to use Nvidia chips when creating the games. In addition to support, Nvidia gave developers new features to use for free, such as better water rendering, which was a major breakthrough at the time. All they asked was that developers add a "Nvidia: The way it's meant to be played" sticker to their package. While perhaps not as big as Intel Inside, it helped reinforce Nvidia as the top-tier graphics card brand in the mind of gamers.

Enemy #3: ATI and the NV30 Debacle

After the demise of 3dfx and holding off Intel, the next enemy for Nvidia was ATI, based in Ontario, Canada. They would go head-to-head with ATI in the graphics chip war for years.

In 2000, ATI was working on a new chip called the R300, which it planned to release on a dedicated graphics card, the Radeon 9700 PRO.

Meanwhile, Nvidia was developing its own new chip, the NV30. Both companies were working to optimize performance for Microsoft's new Direct3D 9 API, scheduled for release in 2002. Direct3D is a critical component in both Xbox and Windows computers and is used extensively in the development of video games. Any graphics chip needed to work flawlessly with it to perform.

But Nvidia was locked in a legal dispute with Microsoft over its new vendor agreement terms around information sharing and intellectual property rights. Since Nvidia refused to sign Microsoft's contract they had to design their chip without access to Direct3D's new technical specs.

ATI signed the agreement with Microsoft and was able to fully optimize its chip, launching it on time in August 2002 for the back-to-school season.

Nvidia's NV30 chip was a major debacle. The chip was delayed five months and still performed poorly. To boost performance, they turned up the clock speed, which led to excessive heat and efficiency issues. To keep it cool they added a huge dual-slot fan over the chip that made a loud, high-pitched noise when activated. Interestingly, noise was not one of the criteria used in their virtual reviews.

The excessively noisy fan became a constant complaint and running joke in the gaming community. To salvage a small shred of the company's reputation, the marketing team suggested posting a spoof video called "The Decibel Dilemma" about the fan noise. If you mess up, it is best to be the first to make fun of yourself.

The video featured four members of the Nvidia product and marketing team discussing how they intended the fan to be loud and were proud of it. It was made to be loud like a Harley-Davidson, could be used as a leaf-blower, and was so hot you could grill on it! The video ends with one of the guys asking, "But do you think a few of the people might think it is too noisy? Nah. Ship it."[13]

The "Decibel Dilemma" video helped to save face with the enthusiasts Nvidia worked so hard to win over. It also stopped ATI from bringing up the noise issue; if they did consumers would see Nvidia's video response as a top link.

However, it was a major low point that was difficult to recover from. "The NV30 disaster almost killed us," Dan Vivoli recalled.

No company is perfect. When you make a mistake, it is best to own it, learn from it, and work hard to never let it happen again. Luckily, Nvidia did all three.

In 2006, AMD acquired ATI in a deal valued at $5.4 billion.[14] AMD later dropped the ATI name and uses the better Radeon name on its graphics cards.

Using GPUs for Supercomputing

In 2000, Ian Buck, a graduate student at Stanford studying computer graphics, chained 32 Nvidia GeForce cards together to play Quake. While very cool, he next wondered if GeForce cards might be useful for other tasks than launching grenades at his friends.

He hacked the cards' primitive programming shaders to access the parallel-computing circuits and repurposed the GeForce into a low-budget supercomputer. Word spread to Jensen Huang, and soon after Buck was working at Nvidia.

Buck led the development of Nvidia's supercomputing software. While Buck did the software, Nvidia's hardware team began allocating space on the microchips for supercomputing capabilities.

In late 2006, Nvidia released CUDA, which stands for Compute Unified Device Architecture. CUDA is a parallel computing platform that allows software developers to tell the GPU to do general-purpose processing. Why is this cool? The GPU excels in tasks that can be parallelized, which improves performance for applications such as scientific simulations, machine learning, and video processing. It allows developers to harness the parallel processing power of the GPU for a wide range of tasks beyond gaming graphics to other things that require intensive data processing.

Changing the Focus for the Future

Revolutionary ideas don't always get off the ground right away; to be the pioneer takes vision, patience, and a bit of luck. While Nvidia was setting itself up to bring supercomputing to the masses, initially there was no indication they wanted it yet.

Ben Gilbert, the co-host of *Acquired*, a popular Silicon Valley podcast, said, "They were spending many billions targeting an obscure corner of academic and scientific computing, which was not a large market at the time—certainly less than the billions they were pouring in."[15]

Strong leadership is essential to ensure a company maintains focus and practices patience. While many thought Nvidia was nuts, Huang's confidence and decisiveness in what they were fighting for and the new category they wanted to pioneer inspired his team to stay the course.

Huang pressed for CUDA to be on every GPU chip, so it would be available and ready to go. He was making a bet on a GPU supercomputing future. Building this new category would take courage too. By the end of 2008, Nvidia's stock price had declined by 70 percent.

Nvidia tried marketing CUDA to a wide range of customers from stock traders to oil prospectors to frozen pizza makers; it wasn't working to move the needle much. Then academic researchers stumbled upon an overlooked use case: neural networks. Neural networks are computing structures inspired by the human brain. Most thought they were outdated and didn't work—until two students, Alex Krizhevsky and Ilya Sutskever at the University of Toronto, used two CUDA-powered chips to do something incredible.

Google had recently trained a neural network to identified videos of cats, an effort that required 16,000 CPUs. The two grad students in Toronto produced similar results with just two Nvidia GPU circuit boards in their bedroom. Huang was intrigued. He foresaw that deep learning could be a big deal and not just a passing fad for cat videos. And he was willing to bet the future of the company on it.

"Jensen sent out an e-mail on Friday evening saying everything is going to deep learning, and that we were no longer a graphics company," recalled Greg Estes, a vice-president at Nvidia. "By Monday morning, we were an AI company. Literally, it was that fast."[16] As of 2013, deep learning would be the new focus for Nvidia.

The Current Focus: World Leader in AI Computing

Slowly deep learning started to gain traction. In 2016, Nvidia donated a supercomputer to the startup OpenAI to work on AI's "toughest problems."[17] The gift led to OpenAI launching ChatGPT in 2022, the first and most famous generative AI tool. Supercomputing had finally come to the masses, and it was powered by Nvidia.

Nvidia's GPUs are the essential component of most deep learning networks. Nvidia's AI platform powers the leading cloud services such as Amazon's AWS, Google Cloud, and Microsoft's Azure.

"AI is pushing the limits of what's possible—turning yesterday's dreams into today's reality," Huang said.[18] Yesterday's wise decisions is what turned Nvidia's dreams into reality, especially Huang's change of focus for Nvidia back in 2013. Changing your anchor is best done swiftly, decisively, and early to pioneer a new category. As a result, Nvidia is now synonymous with AI computing and is the dominant global leader of today's most important computing category.

What About Gaming, the Name, and the Visual Hammer?

While Nvidia's focus shifted to AI over a decade ago, they are still the gold standard when it comes to gaming graphics chips. Changing the anchor to AI didn't require getting rid of gaming; it only required not mentioning it as much. An anchor should be singular. And if you are the leader in AI, consumers will still believe you make top-tier graphics chips. Nvidia knowingly sacrificed being synonymous with the graphics category to pioneer and dominate the AI one.

Nvidia as a name is unique, but it is hard to pronounce, spell, and remember. The proper pronunciation is en-VID-ee-uh. Not everybody gets this right. In the early years, it was a challenge. They should have considered renaming the company before they went public. After the stock was public, the brand was established, and several leaders got Nvidia tattoos, it's much more difficult to make a change.

What made the name stick in the mind of gamers was the success of the GPU category, and today the name is cemented in the mind by the success of AI. Pioneering a new category will help a weak name. But just remember, if your brand is struggling to get off the ground and your name is a hinderance, don't fight it, change it.

In terms of a visual hammer, Nvidia has a green logo with an eye. While the singular color makes it memorable, does the eye communicate anything to you? I doubt it. In the mind, Nvidia is more likely to be remembered by the image of Jensen Huang in his black leather jacket. Founders like Steve Jobs of Apple, Jeff Bezos of Amazon, or Mark Zuckerberg of Meta can be powerful visual hammers, especially when they have a distinctive style.

Core Concepts: Nvidia: A Positioning Success Story

- Saying no is critical; it keeps you focused.
- Mistakes happen; learn from them.
- It takes courage to pioneer a new category.
- Applying the principles of positioning drives company success.

Chapter 10

Leadership Is Your Anchor

Leadership in a category is the most powerful position to own. When it comes to the enemy, leaders will face many. Your pioneering idea will soon be met with competition. You need to be ready for enemies that will attack you from new categories, alternative positions, different price points, and more. Your anchor is leadership in your category; your mission is to defend it. Your job is to aggressively grow the category itself.

Are you a leader? Don't forget your anchor; it maintains your ship's position.

■ ■ ■

When you are the leader, the category is your anchor and what you are fighting for. This can be easy to forget. As your brand name becomes synonymous with your category, it gains power. If you have given your brand a visual hammer, it evokes emotion and creates distinctiveness. You will eventually fall in love with your brand and your consumers will too. The danger then lies in being blinded by love and neglecting the anchor that gives your brand its true meaning.

Too many believe that an anchor is limiting. That it holds you down. The opposite is true. With a strong anchor, you are powerful. The category ship is yours. Your job is to increase interest in the category and to expand not the brand but your distribution globally. With power comes opportunity.

What brands have the most potential to become a global brand? The ones that dominate categories. The leading pasta of Italy—Barilla. The leading oat milk—Oatly. The leading vacuum—Dyson. The leading EV—Tesla. The leading coffee shop—Starbucks.

With an anchor, your job is not to chase but to attract. You need to lead your category with unwavering clarity, confidence, and conviction. This will require investment and courage.

First investment. Brands that are first in new categories benefit from PR and word of mouth. In the early years, there is plenty of talk and attention about your hot new category and brand. This will fade and imitators will swarm in like bees to honey. The time comes when you need to switch to advertising.

Advertising is tremendously important in maximizing the presence of your brand in the marketplace and in the mind. It works best when you have a memorable and consistent message along with a visual hammer. It doesn't just have to be traditional advertising either, but events, in-store displays, sponsorships, and more. You need your brand to be seen more than any other competitor, on the shelf, on the street, and online to keep your brand on top.

Investment should not only go to marketing but be used to improve your product or service as well. You need to keep constantly improving and outdoing even yourself on quality and innovation. Don't let your enemies get an upper hand in your own category.

Second courage. Categories take time to grow. Don't lose patience. Keep the long game in mind. Too often companies don't have enough confidence in the future potential of their own category. They are too quick to expand the brand into other categories instead of expanding interest in the one they own. Just as dangerous, perhaps more so, line extensions will divert time, attention and resources away from maintaining and expanding your original category anchor.

Not all category anchors last forever. Sometimes you might pull up on the anchor and make a radical turn in direction. This can only work, however, if you are first and not a follower. And you need to do it swiftly and confidently, like Jensen did at NVIDIA.

Remember, an anchor doesn't limit you or your future growth potential; there is always the option to keep one category anchor and then drop a second or third anchor by launching a new brand in a new category.

Dude Wipes Wises Up

Dude Wipes greatly benefited from the COVID crazed motivation that drove us all to hoard and buy as much toilet paper as we could get our hands on. Sales jumped to $40 million in 2020 from $15.5 million the previous year. As prospects grabbed any item off the shelf, many discovered and fell in love with Dude Wipes.

But even before the pandemic sales exploded, love for the Dude brand had already put stars in founder Sean Riley's eyes. Dude's rapid growth and brand adoration led him to dream about all sorts of new Dude potential.

In 2019, Sean decided his growing Dude brand should not limit itself to just selling wipes. They should leverage their momentum and transform Dude into an all-natural men's grooming empire. In March 2020, Dude deodorant and Dude Soap were launched.

It was a mistake. Sean shared with me that he read my dad's book *The 22 Immutable Law of Marketing* shortly after the Dude extensions launched. After a few chapters, it hit him like a ton of poop. "Oh Shit! We are making a big mistake."[1]

Big companies rarely admit mistakes. Not Sean. The laws of marketing led him to understand the real opportunity the Dude brand was on the cusp of achieving. Leadership in wipes. To attain it, it would require all his Dude time, resources, and attention.

Leadership Is Your Anchor

"We realized fighting one war with Big Toilet Paper was enough. Trying to compete with Axe, Old Spice, and others would spread us too thin. Consumers prefer category kings who stay in their lanes. They'd rather buy soap from brands like Dr. Squatch, which specialize in it. Competing there wasn't the right move for us. These mistakes early on helped us refocus."

COVID represented a huge opportunity for the brand. Dude quickly ditched the deodorant and soap and doubled down on wipes. They cranked up manufacturing and fired up their marketing machine. It paid off big time. In 2025, Dude Wipes is expected to exceed $300 million in annual sales.

Nike Returns to Its Anchor

When you hear a company say they need to refocus and go back to the basics—it's just another way of saying they took their leadership anchor for granted and expanded away from it too much.

Nike CEO Elliott Hill, who took the helm in October 2024, is intent on restoring Nike's focus on sports and winning. "Let's see more of Nike being Nike," Hill said. "We lost our obsession with sport. Moving forward, we will lead with sport and put the athlete at the center of every decision. The sharpness in each sport is what differentiates our brand and our business and fuels our culture."[2]

During the 2025 Super Bowl, Nike sent a message to the world. They wanted to win us back. Nike's 60-second commercial featured female athletes and was voiced by rapper Doechii. The theme: So Win. "You can't flex. So, flex. You can't dominate. So, dominate. You can't win. So Win." A first step in the right direction.

Starbucks Returns to Its Anchor

Over time companies tend to lose focus. Which is what happened to Starbucks when they added automation, a confusing rewards program, and lots and lots of menu items. Printed labels were efficient but using them reduced the personal barista touch of a Sharpie message customers enjoyed. Even if your name was not spelled correctly.

New Starbucks CEO Brian Niccol is doing his best to bring back the buzz with his "Back to Starbucks" vision that emphasizes coffee and the in-store experience. Turnaround plans include a major reinvestment in marketing and advertising to get the word out that the Starbucks you love is back.

"Back to Starbucks" is exactly as it sounds. Starbucks is going back to the basics of what the brand stands for: coffee. The new ads are focused on the personal touches of Starbucks service and baristas. The ads end with "The Starbucks Coffee Company" after years of shortening the name to just Starbucks and in some cases just the logo. Using the full name and saying "coffee" is important to the company, the employees, and the consumer. Not that they always need to use it, but they should never forget that coffee is the category and what the brand stands for.

Niccol has been making significant changes that include cutting the menu by roughly 30 percent and buying 200,000 Sharpies to bring the chain back it its roots.[3]

"As part of our plan to get back to Starbucks, we're simplifying our menu to focus on fewer, more popular items, executed with excellence," Niccol says. "This will make way for innovation, help reduce wait times, improve quality and consistency, and align with our core identity as a coffee company."[4] Coffee is the anchor of Starbucks; they are wise not to forget it.

Siete: The Grain-Free Mexican Anchor

Veronica Garza was born and raised in the border town of Laredo as a third-generation Mexican-American. As a teenager, she was diagnosed with multiple debilitating autoimmune conditions. At her brother's urging, Veronica adopted the Paleo diet, which is especially helpful in reducing inflammation. Going Paleo meant no more grains, dairy, refined sugars, or legumes—basically, no Mexican food. A bummer. To support Veronica, the whole Garza family did Paleo too. But the fajitas and tacos the family used to enjoy didn't taste the same wrapped in a lettuce leaf.

Instead of settling for lettuce, Veronica created her own tortillas out of almond flour, instead of the wheat flour typically used. She worked on her recipe for over a year until she even got her abuela's stamp of approval on the taste.

Her brother Miguel thought his sister's grain-free tortillas were not just delicious but also had all the ingredients of a solid business idea. Together, they founded Must B Nutty grain-free tortillas, the name was a nod to their main ingredient: almond flour.

In 2014, Must B Nutty hit the shelf of a Food Co-op in Austin for $12 a dozen. Some thought it was a nutty idea, especially at that price. It wasn't. By the next day, they were sold out. Within six months, Must B Nutty grain-free tortillas beat out milk, eggs, and yogurt to become the top-selling item in the fridge section.

But let's be honest. No matter how great the grain-free tortillas were, with Must B Nutty as the name could it become a billion-dollar brand? I doubt it. Names matter.

The Garzas got lucky. In 2016, they were accepted into the Beyond-SKU Food & Beverage Accelerator in New York. The 12-week program provides mentorship, branding guidance, and investor access. A new name, "Siete," was chosen to represent the seven members of the Garza family. It was perfect—an authentic nod to their Latino heritage and family unity in supporting Veronica and her grain-free diet.

Following the rebrand, things took off. When you combine a great product that pioneers a new category with the right positioning, name, and visual hammer, magic happens. Siete grain-free tortillas took off in Whole Foods and expanded nationally.

Over the next several years, Siete expanded into other grain-free and Paleo products such as tortilla chips, taco shells, dairy-free queso, churro strips, and seasonings. Expanding into more grain-free items is what a leader like Siete should do. Grain-Free Mexican foods is their anchor.

In 2022, Siete partnered with a renowned tortilla-focused restaurant in Austin, Texas, called Nixta Taqueria. The name "Nixta" is short for nixtamalización—the ancient Mesoamerican process of soaking corn in an alkaline solution to enhance its nutrition, texture, and flavor—a method that defines the restaurant's tortillas.

As cool as these corn tortillas sound, corn is a grain. Siete is grain-free. They fell in love with their brand and lost sight of their anchor. If anything, these cool Nixta tortillas deserved their own brand instead of getting lost as a line extension under Siete.

Don't feel too bad. In November 2024, PepsiCo announced its $1.2 billion deal for Siete. The Garzas did great. But with PepsiCo in control of the ship now, they are abandoning the anchor and promoting Siete as just another brand.

Athletic Brewing: The Alcohol-Free Beer Anchor

The idea of a beer for a better tomorrow came to Bill Shufelt, a former hedge fund trader, while working long hours on Wall Street. He wanted to enjoy the craft beer he loved without the hangovers that came along with it. While there were plenty of nonalcoholic (NA) beers on the market, the taste didn't meet his flavor standards, and the brands didn't reflect his active lifestyle. "We had to totally change the product and the marketing," Shufelt told the *Wall Street Journal*.[5]

He recruited John Walker, an experienced brewer, and together they teamed up to start the Athletic Brewing Company in 2014. They sought to create a high-quality craft beer without alcohol. To do it, they would need an innovative approach.

At first glance, you might assume NA beer is simply regular beer, minus the alcohol. It's not that simple; the steps to produce NA beer are more technical and complicated than making traditional beer. And without the alcohol buzz numbing the senses and taste buds, consumers pay extra attention to the taste.

The focus was NA craft beer. The name "Athletic" was chosen to reflect the active lifestyle of its customers. Athletic only comes in cans. Its signature brew, Run Wild IPA, comes in a turquoise can.

All other NA beers are primarily sold or at least marketed as coming in glass bottles. Glass communicates premium. But to compete with these brands such as O'Doul's and Heineken 0.0, it is best to do the opposite.

Cans are also more environmentally friendly and better fit the active lifestyle Athletic appeals to. Cans are easy to take the pool, beach, hiking, and more. While other NA beers are available in cans, for Athletic the can is their focus and visual hammer.

But before advertising could come into play, the brand needed credentials. As with wines, winning beer awards deliver great credentials.

And Athletic has been winning a whole lot of them. In 2020, at the International Beer Challenge, Athletic Brewing won the top prize across all North American brewers (alcoholic and nonalcoholic) and was named "Brewer of the Year."[6] These awards and the PR that followed have been creating a lot of buzz for this new NA brew.

In 2024, it was time to fan these flames with advertising. The slogan: "It's Athletic. Ask for it." Athletic is a proud award-winning NA beer. It's the only brew you can order as a NA brew by name. Asking for an Athletic is asking for the real thing, not a substitute. With a name like Heineken 0.0, it will never taste as good as the original. Not to mention it turns their original brand into the enemy.

In 2024, Athletic Brewing exceeded $90 million in sales, according to the company. While that number is small compared to big brewers, the NA category is the fastest growing in the industry and Athletic is leading way. Athletic is the No.1 nonalcoholic beer brand by sales in US grocery stores.[7] Athletic has dropped the anchor, now they need to expand the NA category to even greater success.

Note: In the United States, you are allowed to label your beer "alcohol-free" and still have up to 0.5% ABV (alcohol by volume). Athletic Brews have 0.4% ABV, same as many kombuchas. Heineken is different with its 0.0 approach, but it is saddled with a line-extension name.

Mark Spain: The Guaranteed Cash Offer Anchor

Mark Spain is a second-generation realtor based in Alpharetta, Georgia. He took over his father's ReMax sales team in 1997. Then he joined Keller Williams in 2011 to form his own "Mark Spain" team. In 2015, they had become the No. 1 sales team in the southeast for Keller Williams. He could have stayed put and had a very successful career, but he didn't. He left Keller Williams in 2016 to captain his own ship.

"It's time to continue to expand upon what I have already built and grow my own brand and brokerage," Spain is quoted in the press release announcing his new independent Mark Spain Real Estate company.[8]

His new firm would theoretically have placed him as a top 25 real estate company in metro Atlanta. But he had even bigger aspirations: going national.

At this point, what he did not have was a focus. The press release summarized the brand this way: "Mark Spain Real Estate specializes in assisting metro Atlanta home buyers and sellers in all price points. The group has more combined experience than any other real estate team in metro Atlanta."

Helping home buyers and sellers in all price points? That's not a focus he could use to build a national brand. What took the Mark Spain brand to the next level was establishing a powerful new category in the mind and clearly communicating it.

In 2018, Mark Spain launched his Guaranteed Offer program and has focused on it ever since. The program goes like this: If a seller's home meets certain requirements, Mark Spain will extend an offer. It's basically selling your home without ever having to put it on the market. It eliminates showings, open houses, and an unknown waiting period before an offer is received.

In industry speak, Mark Spain focused on being an "iBuyer," short for instant buyer. Instant buyers use artificial intelligence to determine a home's value, then buy it directly from the owner in all cash for a quick and easy sale. But iBuyer isn't a consumer-friendly idea, which is why Mark Spain communicates it with his Guaranteed Offer program. And especially his list of nos: No Showings. No Open Houses. No Stress.

There are several players in the market now including Opendoor, Zillow Offer, and Offerpad. So recently he made his offer more specific. After accepting the offer, Mark Spain promotes: "You can close in as little as 21 days. Start packing."

What about the homes that don't meet the offer requirement? Does Mark Spain lose all these leads? No. If a home doesn't meet the program parameters, they pair you with a Mark Spain listing agent and sell the home the old-fashioned way—promising to minimize showings while maximizing your home's profit, same as other agents. The catch is they never, ever promote this.

Mark himself is the visual hammer. His face is on every billboard, and he stars in every commercial. As of 2025, Mark Spain has

Leadership Is Your Anchor

expanded to 6 states, 16 markets with over 400 agents, and they sell 33 homes a day on average. Mark Spain is on the way to building a national brand with his Guaranteed Offer anchor.

Netflix: Changes Its Anchor from DVD-by-Mail to Streaming

If you are like me, you remember Netflix's original anchor fondly. Netflix was founded in 1997 by Reed Hastings and Marc Randolph as a DVD-by-Mail rental service. Consumers could pick from tens of thousands of movie titles at Netflix.com and then they mailed the DVD to you in a red envelope. We all ran to the mailbox waiting for the red envelopes to arrive.

Netflix was an innovator from the start. They added monthly subscription plans which included unlimited rentals, no due dates, no late fees, and no shipping costs. The website offered up personalized movie recommendations. It was a wiz in knowing what movie you should rent next. Remember, this was the dawn of the Internet, we were easily impressed.

The enemy was Blockbuster. They were big, arrogant and dominated the home rental market with locations in nearly every neighborhood. Early on Blockbuster could have bought Netflix but didn't. A former high-ranking Blockbuster exec at the time recalled, "We had the option to buy Netflix for $50 million, and we didn't do it. They were losing money."[9] Hindsight is always 20/20, but when you are as profitable as Blockbuster was at that time, management has a hard time accepting a niche technology could sink your ship.

In 2007, Netflix launched its streaming service. At no additional cost, they allowed subscribers to instantly watch movies and television shows on their personal computer. They gave it away for free to induce trial which accelerated the growth of this new category.

It was the dawn of a new era. By 2011, Netflix had consumers hooked and they were ready to ditch the DVD anchor for the streaming anchor. First, they split the subscription plans, which effectively raised the prices for subscribers of both DVD and streaming by 60 percent. About a million customers or 4 percent of subscribers cancelled their accounts. But this ship was captained by a strong leader.

CEO Reed Hastings got even bolder. Later that year, he announced plans to spin off the DVD-by-mail business and rebrand it Qwikster. It was the right strategy, but it was met with such bad press and backlash from both consumers and Wall Street, that they abandoned the plans a few weeks later.

For investors, the problem with spinning off the DVD-by-mail service was that it represented 44 percent of the revenue and the DVD revenue per subscriber was substantially higher than for the streaming service. In 2011 Q4, Netflix had 11.1 million DVD subscribers, which represented revenues of $370 million. While the number of streaming subscribers for that quarter were nearly double, at 21.6 million, they only generated revenues of $476 million.[10]

For users it came down to the account login. People didn't want to use two different websites and with two different user accounts.

Hastings issued a mea culpa: "Consumers value the simplicity Netflix has always offered and we respect that. There is a difference between moving quickly—which Netflix has done very well for years—and moving too fast, which is what we did in this case."[11]

No doubt, Hastings said this through gritted teeth. Netflix was smart to move fast, he knew that. The problem wasn't the strategy; it was the big announcement and weird Qwikster name. In 2012, Netflix quietly bought the DVD.com domain and slowly moved all the accounts and changed the red envelopes to say DVD.com, a Netflix company.

To the press, Reed Hastings made it clear that the company would focus on streaming only. "DVD will do whatever it's going to do," he said at media conference. "We're going to try to not hurt it, but we're not putting a lot of time and energy into doing anything particular around it."[12] When DVD.com was shut down in 2023, few realized it was even still available.

With its new anchor firmly in place, Netflix continued to take steps to strengthen it. In 2013, they began producing original content. *House of Cards* was its first big hit and garnered numerous awards, including three Primetime Emmy Awards in its first season.

Leadership Is Your Anchor

In 2023, Netflix began livestreaming with *Chris Rock: Selective Outrage*. The stand-up special, which aired a week before the Oscars, was Rock's first public response after Will Smith slapped him at the Oscars the year before.

According to the *New York Times*, "Rock said there are four ways people can get attention in our culture: showing your ass, being infamous, being excellent, or playing the victim. It's a good list, but this special demonstrates a conspicuous omission: nothing draws a crowd like a fight."[13] So true.

Core Concepts: Leadership Is Your Anchor

- An anchor represents leadership in a category.
- Leadership is the most powerful position to own in the mind.
- Leaders should expand the category, not the brand.
- Leaders need to be prepared to face many enemies.

Chapter 11

Giving Birth to Your Own Enemy

No category lives forever, and new categories are being born all the time. The best way to ensure the future success of your company is to launch new brands in new categories to become your own enemy. If anyone is going to launch a brand to compete with you, it might as well be you.

■ ■ ■

Too many companies fall in love with their brand. It's the reason line extending brands is so popular. But consumers don't love brands; they love categories. Brands are just how they verbalize categories. Instead of line extensions, companies should be on the lookout to be first in new categories with a new brand.

However, since new categories start small, often they don't appear to be a big deal in the beginning. A line extension is a tempting way to stick your toe into the new category. But if the category takes off, brands with a narrow focus will have the advantage. And your line-extended brand will be forced to manage one brand across diverging categories, which isn't easy.

Worse still, if your brand's main category is going downhill, line extensions can't save you. They will dig the hole faster. Your loser brand will be on the old as well as the new category. For example, Kodak should have given birth to its own enemy. The opportunity was for a consumer digital camera that strongly attacked film photography as the enemy. Kodak had the advantage by launching the first digital camera but saddled it with a line extension name. Kodak eventually lost out in both the old and the new categories. The best defensive move is to launch a second brand positioned for the future.

Verde Valle Gives Birth to Isadora

Founded in 1967 in Guadalajara, Verde Valle is king of beans and rice in Mexico. At the time, rice and beans were a commodity that producers sold to wholesalers. Verde Valle did the opposite. Founder Sergio Rosales's vision was twofold. First, he wanted to work directly with farmers to buy the freshest crops right from the fields to ensure the highest quality and most nutritious food product. Second, he wanted to take what had been a commodity and turn it into a consumer-targeted brand. Verde Valle focused on selling to grocery stores and building the Verde Valle brand directly with consumers.

When it comes to their success, like most companies they talk about the quality of the product over having a great name and being first. "Our main value to our consumers is that we try and provide the best quality product possible, and that has been the reason for our success," said Ricardo Castellanos, Verde Valle's manager of international sales, in 2016. "Our beans come from the freshest harvest, and our rice is considered the fluffiest and cleanest."[1]

Despite the strength of the brand, the company's internal research showed that consumers felt it was not up-to-date. While consumers trusted Verde Valle, they considered it a "traditional brand" and the "brand your mother buys."

Clients don't usually hire us unless there is a problem and/or an opportunity. Verde Valle was faced with both.

My dad and I started working with Verde Valle back in 2003. Verde Valle was the leading brand and was priced 10–20 percent higher than the competition; all the other brands had to sell on price to compete. Both the beans and the rice products had around 23 percent market share. But there was a category cloud on the horizon and the company wasn't sure what to do.

A Category in Decline: Dry Beans

From 1993 to 2003, the average per-capita consumption of beans in Mexico had fallen from 35 pounds a year to only 24 pounds. That's a decline of 31 percent. It was a shocking statistic for Verde Valle since bean sales represented more than half of their business.

There were several reasons for this decline. Cooking dried beans requires 55 minutes in a pressure cooker. As more women in Mexico were working and had less time to cook, many were switching to convenient products such as canned beans, pasta, and even noodles in cups. Beans are a staple of Mexican cuisine; they are also a super-healthy food filled with fiber and protein. Verde Valle wanted to protect their business as well as their culture. But how could they get people to eat more beans?

Cooked beans in a can are a convenient alternative to cooking them yourself. But the reality as well as the perception was that canned beans didn't taste as good as home-cooked beans. As a result, younger consumers cut back on eating beans all together, unless they went to Grandma's and she cooked them.

They had already tried to launch a canned bean brand using the Verde Valle name. This line extension was a loser and in fifth place. Why? For starters there were already well-known leaders in the canned beans category. Plus, the quality perception as the leader in dry beans was not carried over into the canned bean category. In the consumer's mind, just because you can put quality dried beans in a bag doesn't mean you are any good at cooking them and putting them in a can.

A New Category: Cooked Beans-in-a-Pouch

Verde Valle shared research with us on new technology they were working on to produce ready-to-eat food in pouches. They tested bean recipes and found the taste was superior to canned products. This was an amazing opportunity to be the first brand to use this revolutionary new packaging.

Instead of convincing more people to cook beans, a new cooked-beans-in-a-pouch brand was a better solution to reverse declining bean consumption. It provided all the convenience of the canned product with the taste of home-cooked beans.

A New Name for the New Category

Verde Valle is the name most Mexicans trusted for dry beans. Beans-in-a-pouch would taste like home-cooked beans, and they would be first in this new category. What name would you use for the product? Most consultants would have recommended they use Verde Valle; the company was strongly considering that direction too.

This was a new category with enormous potential in the long term. My dad and I convinced Verde Valle that it demanded a new brand name. The company launched the first cooked beans-in-a-pouch brand using the name Isadora in 2004.

The enemy was beans in a can. Isadora ran advertising showing teeth covered in tin cans, strongly positioning Isadora as the bean brand that didn't have the notorious tin can taste. While the message was extremely powerful, shifting consumer behavior from one category to another takes time.

In this case it took a decade. In 2015, the sales of beans in a pouch outsold beans in a can. By 2024, 72 percent of beans were sold in pouches, and only 28 percent in cans. Isadora is of course the dominant brand.

German Rosales Wybo, CEO of Verde Valle, fondly remembers that challenging meeting and tough decision on the name for his new beans-in-a-pouch product. "Al and Laura advised us: If you're going to open a new category, use a new brand. We weren't sure, but we trusted the advice and Isadora was born. Back then it was hard to imagine the pouch category ever being bigger than cans, but it is, and we are the leaders."

The success of Isadora made Verde Valle a stronger and more profitable company. It had a halo effect on all the company's brands. Verde Valle's market share in dry rice and beans continues to increase and is currently over 30 percent.

Campbell's Gives Birth to Prego

In a sense, the Verde Valle brand, is a traditional brand much like Campbell's soup, the powerful brand that dominates the condensed soup market. Consumers also consider Campbell's soup the "traditional brand" and a "brand your mother buys." Today, Campbell's is more like the brand your grandmother bought.

Despite spending several hundreds of millions of dollars on advertising, Campbell's has been unable to change the perception of being a traditional brand and had little success using it on anything besides condensed soup. It's an important principle to remember. The more established your brand is, the more difficult it is to change the brand's perception in the mind.

In 1981, the company planned to introduce Campbell's Very Own Spaghetti Sauce. Advertising executive Laurel Cutler convinced Campbell's to change the name to Prego. The day before the client meeting, Laurel scanned an English-Italian dictionary and plucked out "prego," which means both "please" and "you're welcome."[2]

Prego successfully took on the leader, Ragu, with television commercials that visually compared how much thicker Prego sauce was—something that would have been a tough sell with a soup name like Campbell's. I can only hope the final slides of Laurel's presentation said, "You're welcome for this brilliant multibillion-dollar idea."

Gap Gives Birth to Old Navy

The Gap was founded in 1969 by Don Fisher and his wife Doris with a simple idea: make it easier to find a pair of jeans that fit. As the story goes, Don ordered a pair of Levi's in the wrong size and couldn't find a local store to exchange them at. So, he opened his own store in San Francisco, in the midst of the hippie movement, and sold a wide range of Levi's jeans alongside records and tapes. Don wanted to call it "Pants and Discs," but his wife came up with a better name: "The Gap," shorthand for "generation gap."

The brand capitalized on the rise of denim as the go-to look for a generation of young Americans and then expanded into other basics such as khakis, T-shirts, and hoodies. Under the masterful leadership of Mickey Drexler, who joined in 1983, the brand became an American icon. By 1990, Gap sales were just shy of $2 billion and there were 1,092 Gap brand stores. Drexler dropped the Levi's brand in 1991 to focus exclusively on Gap denim, further cementing the brand. In 1992, supermodels wearing Gap white denim jeans and white shirts graced the cover of *Vogue* magazine's 100th anniversary issue.

The Gap brand symbolized cool and casual style. "As ubiquitous as McDonald's, as centrally managed as the former Soviet Union and as American as Mickey Mouse, the Gap Inc. has you covered, from the cradle to the grave," the *New York Times* said in 1992.[3] The brand won over everyone from moms to office workers to celebrities like Sharon Stone, who wore a black Valentino skirt and a $26 mock Gap turtleneck to the Academy Awards in 1996.

It was at the height of this success that Drexler launched a new brand, Old Navy. A brand that would one day overtake the original.

Old Navy Was Almost Gap Warehouse

Drexler's concept was to launch a value brand that was focused on affordable fashion for everyone. The prototype name for the store was "Gap Warehouse." It was a name many companies would have used, attempting to capitalize on the strength of the original. But they didn't. Two individuals brands, each with their own identity and focus, was better.

If they had called it Gap Warehouse, initially it would have been fine, and customers would go there to get Gap clothes at cheaper prices. But long-term they would have given birth to their own worst enemy. The Gap would have suffered for not being affordable, and the Gap Warehouse seen as not as good as the original. Not only that, how could each have a distinctive identity when they used the same name? They couldn't.

Instead, they gave birth to a new brand, Old Navy, in 1994. This new brand pioneered the idea that fashion didn't have to be just for rich people; it could be for everyone. Within four years, Old Navy reached $1 billion in sales, the fastest brand ever to do so.

By 2000, Gap Inc. had three strong brands and achieved its highest market capitalization at $43.4 billion.[4] The store count was 2,548 for Gap, 666 for Old Navy.

The numbers don't tell the whole story; while Old Navy was smaller, it was the future. It was the dawn of affordable fashion, and Old Navy was leading the way as new competitors such as Zara and H&M were entering the market. Gap launching a second brand early positioned the overall company for success.

In 2005, Old Navy overtook the Gap with $6.9 billion in sales. (Gap was $6.8 billion.) Since then, while the Gap was losing focus, Old Navy has been Gap Inc.'s golden child and top-performing brand. In 2024, Gap Inc. sales were $15.1 billion. Old Navy was $8.4 billion. Gap was $3.3 billion. Banana Republic was $1.9 billion. Athleta was $1.4 billion.[5]

The Fall and Potential Rise of the Gap

Launching Old Navy saved the company. But what about the Gap? The ship needed a strong captain at the helm—one that could keep the brand anchored.

In the 2000s, Gap, spooked by the rise of fast fashion, started churning out trendy clothing instead of the classics it was known for. Drexler left the Gap in 2002. News articles on his departure cited "hip-huggers" and "orchid leather pants and crocheted halter tops"[6] as examples of the Gap's misguided failures.

Gap became stale with always-on-sale apparel. Too many stores, too much merchandise, and a lack of cohesive vision sent them into decline. In a world of fast fashion, they lost their identity. But it wasn't all bad; they still had Old Navy. If anyone is going to overtake some of your market share, it might as well be you.

There is hope for a turnaround for the Gap. New leadership is intent on refocusing and reinvigorating the brand. In 2024, they installed fashion designer Zac Posen as creative director. When asked how Gap could reinvent itself, he answered, "You go back to what you do best."[7]

Posen brings much needed attention, but he has also delivered a much-needed focused approach. While his 53-piece collection of new Gap classics is great, the attention has been much narrower and focused on two key pieces: the white shirt and baggy jeans.

First came the so-called Anne Hathaway white shirt dress, a reinvented take on Gap's iconic white shirt. Zac designed it for Hathaway to wear at a Bulgari event in Rome, and then Gap released a $158 version of the dress that sold out in less than three hours.[8]

Next came a renewed focus on jeans. Gap showcased its fall denim collection with the help of Australian Grammy Award–nominated artist Troye Sivan, called "Get Loose" to promote Gap's new baggy and loose-fit denim.[9] It put a modern spin on the marketing approach that made the brand a 1990s wardrobe staple.

Uniqlo Gives Birth to GU

Japanese apparel giant Uniqlo gave birth to GU back in 2006. Today GU operates 470 stores in Asia, primarily in Japan, but is now going global. In 2024, GU landed in America with a new US e-commerce site and a flagship store in SoHo, New York.

How does GU differ? While Uniqlo is focused on timeless basics, GU is focused on trendy styles. It is a classic situation; as trendy brands like Zara took off, the best strategy was not to extend Uniqlo into trendy, but to launch a new brand and to do it early.

As the GU brand goes global, the enemy is no longer Zara but Shein. Shein focuses on microtrends and is the leader in online fast fashion with super-low pricing. Check out TikTok and #SheinHaul. Consumers love to share how they load up on Shein fashions.

Unlike Shein that will chase any trend, GU focuses only on a few key trends each season and executes them well at a reasonable price.

"GU differentiates itself by taking a different approach to other global fashion brands in the same price range that sell a huge variety of styles by offering less than one-tenth the number of items," GU's spokesperson told *Fast Company*.[10]

In other words, they use the same approach as Uniqlo but focused on trendy items and launched it with a new brand. Expansion isn't a bad strategy; expansion with one brand is the issue. When you launch a new brand, you can have your expansion cake and eat it too.

Celsius Buys Alani Nu

Brands don't always get the focus right on the first try. It isn't just about having a focus; it's about having a focus that is simple, clear, and believable.

Celsius, founded in 2004, was launched as the first thermogenic beverage brand. They claimed it could increase metabolism and cause the body to burn more calories and body fat than would be the case with exercise alone. They had some studies to back it, but it was a hard sell. The company was performing so poorly that it was delisted from Nasdaq in 2012 and removed from major retailers such as Costco where it made most of its revenue. It was a wakeup call and led to a very successful rebranding and refocusing effort.

The cans were simplified with a clean look, and it was positioned as a "functional energy beverage" for consumers into fitness. Celsius's fitness association and branding has led to the brand being basically 50/50 when it comes to men and women consumers. This unisex focus was successful in positioning it against male-oriented energy brands such as Red Bull and Monster. Celsius also didn't try to appeal to everyone; they focused on consumers between the ages of 18 and 24. To these young adults, Red Bull is what their parents drank, and Celsius was for them. Celsius became the drink of choice for college kids to fuel late nights studying, early morning classes, afternoon workouts, and more.

The success of Celsius did not go unnoticed. PepsiCo invested $550 million in 2022, which gave it far wider distribution. Today, Celsius is a billion-dollar brand and is in third place in the energy drink category with 10.6 percent of the market.[11]

But now they are facing a female focused enemy, Alani Nu. Alani Nu's brand targets women from its packaging to its innovative flavors and has a strong social media following that is 92 percent female.

In the first three quarters of 2024, Alani Nu grew 62.7 percent in volume and claimed a 3.5 percent market share. Celsius was up 38 percent. Both Monster and Red Bull were down.

The question is: What should Celsius do about the threat? Make Celsius more girly? Imitate Alani Nu's innovative flavors such as Pink Slush and Orange Kiss with copycat versions? That could risk alienating the 50 percent of Celsius drinkers that are male. And maybe some of the ladies too; not every woman wants a girly drink.

Instead, Celsius announced its $1.8 billion purchase of Alani Nu in February 2025.[12] Many in the beverage industry applauded the acquisition as taking out a fast-growing competitor that had been a threat. The truth is it is the opposite. They will now own the competitor that is still a threat to Celsius. Celsius and Alani Nu will still be enemies, but now both are owned by one company that can keep each brand clearly positioned to maintain maximum category coverage. They are best kept separate and unique. This is the advantage and opportunity of owning multiple competing brands.

The other option would have been for Celsius to launch a new brand to compete with Alani Nu. But they were too late for that option; it was better to just buy them.

Mike's Hard Lemonade Gives Birth to White Claw

No drink is more American than lemonade. Yet Mike's Hard Lemonade was not originally American; it was founded in Vancouver, Canada, by entrepreneur Anthony von Mandl. Initially it was a spiked lemonade spirit drink made with vodka, natural flavorings, and carbonated water; it was reformulated replacing the vodka with fermented malt for distribution in the United States. Malt beverages you can buy at all supermarkets, hard alcohol you cannot, except for in a handful of states.

On April Fools' Day 1999, Mike's Hard Lemonade was introduced in the United States and quickly became a phenomenon, selling two million cases in its first year. The product was made with simple ingredients and natural flavors. Lemon, water, sugar, and a little alcohol. It quickly became popular with female drinkers and young adults looking for a sweeter alternative to beer.

By 2013, Mike's Hard revenue was $500 million. But sales were starting to stagnate. While natural products were on the rise, so was the trend toward low-carb, low-sugar alternatives. A standard 11.2-ounce bottle of Mike's Hard Lemonade contains 220 calories and 33 grams of sugar. A 12-ounce can of Coca-Cola contains 155 calories and 39 grams of sugar. In 2014, they launched Mike's Lite Hard Lemonade, which had 30 percent fewer calories; this cut some sugar but not enough for the keto-crowd.

White Claw Wasn't First in Its Category

In 2016, Mike's gave birth to White Claw. A new brand for a new category. Today White Claw is the dominant brand of hard seltzer with 60 percent market share and more than $2 billion in sales. While many remember it as the first hard seltzer, it wasn't actually first.

If you study history, the winner in a category was not always the first in the market. Meaning, the first-mover advantage is only an advantage if you establish your brand in the mind. Getting into the mind requires building a better brand. Your focus, name, category, and visual hammer are essential; the one that gets the brand positioning right usually is the winner in the mind.

SpikedSeltzer was first. Beverage entrepreneur Nick Shields launched it in 2013. Shields got the idea after seeing women in a dive bar in Westport, Connecticut, ordering vodka sodas one after the other.

Giving Birth to Your Own Enemy

It was positioned as a low-carb cocktail alternative with an alcohol content of 6 percent, 140 calories, and 5 grams of carbs. SpikedSeltzer's dry taste was compared to something between a vodka soda and champagne. It was upscale and came in glass bottles featuring a mermaid logo. Clearly this drink was aimed at the vodka soda ladies crowd. The generic brand name was a problem; spiked seltzer was a category name, not a brand name.

Sales did take off for this new type of low-carb beverage, which was quickly noted by others in the industry. By 2016 two other major brands were launched. One did it similar to SpikedSeltzer, while the other did it differently.

The Boston Beer Company, famous for Samuel Adams, launched Truly Spiked & Sparkling, which also came in a glass bottle. Mike's Hard Lemonade launched White Claw, which came in a slim and tall can.

White Claw Wins

Why did White Claw succeed? They reinvented the category SpikedSeltzer created. They used a better name, a great visual, and differentiated packaging, plus it only had 100 calories, 2 grams of carbs, and 5 percent alcohol.

They combined all this with a decidedly gender-neutral marketing approach. For decades, all alcoholic beverages were either for men or women, never both. Bros drank beer, ladies drank wine. These associations are strongly embedded in the mind and have been proliferated by advertising for decades. Changing a strongly held perception of an established category or brand is nearly impossible.

White Claw from the start showed both men and women on equal footing. "It was entirely intentional," said Sanjiv Gajiwala, vice president of marketing for White Claw. White Claw would be the drink of the new gender norms, of the kinds of "group hangs" that define young people's social lives. "It wasn't a world where guys got together in a basement and drank beer and women were off doing something else, drinking with their girlfriends," Gajiwala said.

"Whatever we put out creatively and how we positioned the brand really reflects that everyone hangs out together all the time."[13]

After White Claw put all the pieces in place, it caught fire with consumers. Word of mouth is essential for any brand and White Claw had it in spades. It wasn't advertising that built the brand; it was PR and buzz. Including a viral video posted by comedian Trevor Wallace that firmly established the brand and coined its unofficial slogan, "Ain't no laws when you're drinking Claws."[14] The brand didn't pay for the video, nor did it endorse the slogan. In fact, they sent Wallace a cease-and-desist after all he did for the brand.

What others say about your brand is important and Trevor summed up the brand better and more honestly than any company could do itself. Some quotes from Trevor's video:

> *"If you think about it, LaCroix is just a virgin White Claw."*
> *"You're a Truly's girl? You probably have an Android too."*
> *"Know what it tastes like? Nothing."*
> *"Like a Perrier that does squats."*
> *"Pretty sure these Claws are healthier that water."*
> *"It's literally gluten-free water that will fuck you up."*
> *"100 calories and 100% down to ..."*
> *"You don't like White Claws? Guess you don't like America."*

Since then, hundreds of competitive hard seltzer brands have flooded the market, from Bud Light Seltzer to Vizzy. In 2019, Spiked-Seltzer was rebranded as Bon & Viv in a flashy Super Bowl commercial. All for naught—it was discontinued in 2023.

Mike's Hard Lemonade made its best move ever by giving birth to a new brand called White Claw. They didn't even invent the category. They just knew how to perfect it and brand it.

High Noon Takes on White Claw

One final note to the story that I can't leave out. There was one brand that has successfully competed against White Claw. In 2019, at the start of the White Claw Summer, E. & J. Gallo Winery launched High Noon. High Noon wasn't a copycat; it was a new category. They approached White Claw as the enemy and did things differently. High Noon uses real vodka. It was an indisputable difference that was easy to understand. Then they combined it with a great name that lent itself to a simple visual. By 2022, High Noon reached $1 billion in sales. It is the leading spirit-based hard seltzer brand and overtook Tito's as the top-selling spirits brand by volume.

What did White Claw do next? Sadly, it launched line extensions, including:

- White Claw Spirits Premium & Flavored Vodka
- White Claw Spirits Vodka+Soda
- White Claw Spirits Tequila Smash
- White Claw Surge with 8% alcohol
- White Claw Zero Proof with no alcohol
- Claw Tails from White Claw in classic cocktail flavors

White Claw isn't just a brand name; it's the can of hard seltzer itself. Putting one name on different categories won't work. It only weakens the brand. When consumers go shopping for a party, what do they typically put in the cart? Brands, yes. But more importantly they think category first and then usually pick the leading brand. For example: White Claw, High Noon, Tito's, Athletic, Budweiser, Modelo Especial, Sam Adams, Coca-Cola, Monster, Evian, LaCroix. Single brands that dominate the category they own. Have you ever seen a cart with one brand and all its line extensions? Not unless they were giving it away on clearance. Don't be that brand.

Your brand needs to stand for something. Only when it stands for something will it have an enemy to fight against. When you build a brand and category as powerful as White Claw has done in hard seltzers, you need to care for your anchor. Growth is best achieved by giving birth to new brand.

> **Core Concepts: Giving Birth to Your Own Enemy**
> - Protect your company's future by launching new brands, in new categories.
> - Instead of expanding your brand, give birth to your own enemy.
> - If anyone is going to compete with you, it might as well be you.
> - The advantage is being first in the mind in a new category.

Chapter 12

Getting Started: Strategy in Action

The principles in this book are simple to understand. The challenge comes when applying them in real life, which is filled with emotional connections to your brand and financial responsibilities to your company. That's the reason why this book is packed with case studies. It's way easier to consider what others should or should not do; of course, Coca-Cola should not have launched Coca-Cola Life. With your own brand you will be tempted by similarly foolish line extensions. Just say no.

Be courageous. Identifying your strategic enemy will bring focus, clarity, and emotional power to your own brand's positioning.

■ ■ ■

Go out and pick your fight. Just remember, the concept of the strategic enemy is not about conflict for conflict's sake. It's about creating a contrast to bring clarity, focus, and commitment to your own brand. Positioning against a clearly defined enemy—whether another competitor, category, or convention—will give your brand the sharpness and emotional charge necessary to cut through the clutter and be accepted into the mind of the prospect to become a brand worth fighting for.

Now it is your turn to apply these principles to your own brand and business. To help get you started, this chapter has a list of key concepts to work on. For inspiration, I have included an example of how we helped Southworks, a B2B client, successfully apply the principles of positioning, the strategic enemy, and visual hammer.

If they can do it, you can too!

You Need to Look into the Mind

Positioning doesn't start with what you want to stand for. It starts with what the prospect is willing to believe. Too many companies make claims; they don't own positions.

Therefore, the first thing to do is to understand what is going on in the mind. What do prospects and consumers think about you? What are the competing brands and categories you face? How are they perceived?

Research helps. Talking to customers and prospects helps. Reading media stories about your brand helps. You need to deepen your understanding of what the consumer already believes. You need to look for what meaningful "holes" exist in their mind that your brand can potentially fill and what differences you can exploit. Positioning is not just about what you will stand for, it's about what you will stand against.

When we started working with Southworks back in 2022, the problem was clear. They did not yet own a clear position in the mind. Like many companies, they were selling a service; but they were not yet building a brand.

Maybe this is where you are. You have an idea, some success, but now you want to get to the next level. Using positioning and the strategic enemy will guide you.

What's a Southworks? Looking at their website: They "Make Everything Right." That's a nice claim, but it's a self-defined one. Claims like this are not believable, especially to a prospect that has never heard of you.

Looking into the mind, we learned Southworks' current customers loved them for solving complex development problems with speed and efficiency. While the business had modest growth from referrals, they wanted to turn up the heat.

What positioning message would entice more prospects to check them out? How could they get customers to more easily share the company's story? How could they best leverage PR? What would make the brand more distinctive? How could they become a brand worth fighting for?

Southworks needed to clearly define their brand and category by being specific about who they were fighting against. Then use the power of a visual hammer to communicate and reinforce it.

You Need a Strategic Enemy

Finding an enemy forces your brand to focus on a specific idea. This focus will energize the company and consumers alike to rally around your cause.

A strategic enemy must be instantly accepted as a worthy adversary. The contrast should be simple and clear. It is best done using an indisputable difference. When this difference can be visualized it's even better. Hard vs. soft. Plastic vs. cans. Square vs. round. Big vs. small. Crunchy vs. soft.

When you start with how you are different from an enemy, it allows you to tell your story and detail why it makes you better. This makes the choice to pick your brand simple and clear.

Southworks was competing with large, medium, and small outsourcing companies in India, Eastern Europe, and the Americas.

They needed to pick a strategic enemy and then position themselves as the alternative. Find a point of difference that would catch the attention of the prospect, something specific that the enemy would be unlikely to add or is unable to change.

Southworks had a number of potential enemy candidates, the challenge was picking the right one; one that set up the clearest distinction in the mind and would be quickly and easily accepted.

For Southworks we identified the strategic enemy as outsourcing companies in India and Eastern Europe that sold development based on long-term contracts.

You Need to Say No

Many times, it is best to start with what you are not, to best communicate what you are. When you say no, it is also instantly believable. When you say you make everything right? Not so much. "That's what they all say," thinks the prospect.

Saying no sends a strong message about what your brand stands for and helps keep the company aligned and sharp. If you say yes to everything it dilutes your brand's message, causes a loss of focus, and makes it harder for consumers to understand what you're fighting against. Saying no will take courage, especially in the face of customer demands and market pressures.

Southworks did indeed have a different system for selling development. They use three-person teams with pricing that is simple, transparent, and predictable. Customers can book them weekly or monthly and pay one flat rate. But the best way to communicate this is to start with all the nos:

- No long-term contracts
- No overhead
- No hidden costs
- No hand-holding
- No do-overs
- No surprises

These are all the pain points Southworks was set up to solve. Prospects reading these are much more inclined to find out more. In particular, no long-term contracts can be instantly visualized by the mind. I know exactly what a contract looks like.

You Need to Define What Category You're In

When a prospect sees your brand, the first thing they try to figure out is: What folder in my mind will I put this in? So, you need to make sure you answer this vital question up front. Maybe it is an existing folder or maybe you are creating a new one. Or maybe it is a bit of both.

Southworks' current category was commonly called nearshore software development. But that category name did not differentiate them.

They had tried using several words to capture the essence of what made them different such as elastic, lean, agile, flexible, just-in-time, and scalable. Many words like agile were used by everybody. The key was to find a new phrase that was sticky, specific, and memorable.

The new category we came up with was: *Development on Demand*.

This sets up the enemy's position as development by contract. Giving the prospect a simple choice. The enemy is not wrong or bad. It is just different. It never hurts to use alliteration; it makes it more memorable. On demand is also an idea used in many other categories, so using it here made it instantly understandable.

You Need to Kick off a Great Debate

Creating a debate engages consumers, stimulates discussion, and fuels word of mouth, which are key drivers of brand success. A debate gives people something specific to talk about and take a stand on. It energizes your brand and helps to sharpen the brand narrative.

To kick off a great debate there need to be two easily understood and defined options or brands that create enough contrast to stimulate the customer's interest and engagement. There must be enough controversy to spark opinions and generate buzz.

In this debate, your brand should stand firmly for a specific idea to rally supporters and motivate people to choose your side. Arm your audience with simple, convincing facts and talking points so they can effectively promote and defend your brand's position in discussions. Customers value authentic, third-party opinions, which is why public relations and word of mouth are so effective.

Doing it Right vs Doing it Wrong, is not a debate.

On Demand Development vs. Long-Term Contracts is debatable.

Getting Started: Strategy in Action

You Need the Right Name and a Visual Hammer

Names are incredibly important. But they are not what you work on first when it comes to positioning. First you decide the strategy, and then you decide if the name is right. Sometimes it is; other times it's not.

Southworks is a terrific name. It connects with two key ideas in the mind, both of which are essential to the brand. "South" refers to where the developers are located: South America. "Works," as in development that works. Together these two ideas make for a distinctive brand name: Southworks.

When it comes to making names memorable, the more connections your name hits in the mind, the better. It is why using words out of context is an effective naming strategy, even when they don't have a connection to what you sell. For example, Star + Bucks. The name is easily understood. But unlike the name Starbucks, Southworks as the name instantly lent itself to the perfect visual hammer.

With a name like Southworks and developers in South America there is no better visual to represent this than a map of South America. The map visual adds emotion and memorability to the idea. It communicates the location of the developers and reinforces the name.

Of course, this brought up the question from the client: What about the 10 percent of developers who are in Central America and Mexico? Listen, there are no visual hammer police checking to see if 100 percent of your developers are in South America. It covers the vast majority, and it is the best way to visualize the name. The color they chose was orange, the singular color they were using already.

You Need Courage

Making bold changes is not easy. It takes courage. It is one of the reasons why companies benefit from consultants. A great consultant should not only work on the strategy but also instill the company with the courage to execute it.

Even with the name Southworks and 90 percent of the developers in South America, the company had downplayed and even hid this fact. It was a US company, selling to US clients. There was concern about looking too foreign. It takes courage to be different.

What they felt was a disadvantage, actually was a key differentiating strength. South America is on the rise as a hotbed for affordable and quality developers. Plus, it is in the same time zone as the US, not 12 hours ahead or behind. Southworks needed to own and celebrate their true authentic roots.

Southworks summoned their courage and used the strategy. And it worked. But don't just take it from me. Here is what Alex Jack, founder of Southworks and Johnny Halife, CEO of Southworks reported back to me two years after our session:

"Working with Laura brought so much clarity. She helped us sharpen our focus by defining what we don't do—our 'list of no's'—and by encouraging us to clearly 'define the enemy.'

She also challenged us to embrace our South American roots instead of downplaying them—and that shift changed everything. The visual hammer gave us a powerful, immediate way to show the world who we are and why it matters. Today, we're proud to be putting South America on the map as a global development hub.

And finally, 'Development on Demand' gave us a simple, memorable way to tell our story. We probably should've called her sooner—but I'm just glad we didn't wait any longer."

There is a magic moment when working on a positioning strategy when the solution suddenly becomes clear. In hindsight, the best strategic moves appear obvious. Perhaps this is the true test of positioning greatness. The reality is these ideas took enormous sweat to construct and tremendous courage to execute.

It has taken me decades of working with positioning to master it. I had the great privilege of learning from the very best there was. My father taught me the importance of being different and contrasting your positioning relative to competitors in the mind. And he often reminded me of how calling out creativity as the enemy played a key role in the launch of positioning itself.

This book was written to honor his legacy and spotlight the strategic enemy as a critical positioning tool. I hope *The Strategic Enemy* can help guide you in building a brand worth fighting for. I'm fighting for you!

Getting Started: Strategy in Action

Notes

Chapter 1

1. See https://www.inc.com/jeff-haden/neuroscience-says-your-brain-craves-new-for-dopamine-rush-but-research-shows-you-can-replace-that-sensation-much-more-productively.html.
2. See https://newsroom.acehardware.com/ace-hardware-ranked-1-in-home-improvement-on-forbes-2025-best-customer-service-list/.

Chapter 2

1. See https://insideevs.com/news/487969/2020-us-electric-car-sales-tesla-share/.
2. See https://caredge.com/guides/electric-vehicle-market-share-and-sales.
3. See https://pitchbook.com/news/articles/pet-food-farmers-dog-profits-more-than-1b-annualized-revenue.

Chapter 3

1. See www.investopedia.com/articles/personal-finance/111015/story-uber.asp.
2. See https://international-aluminium.org/landing/aluminium-facts/.
3. See www.sacra.com/c/liquid-death.
4. See www.inc.com/bryan-elliott/behind-150-million-dude-wipes-brand-with-ceo-sean-riley.html.
5. Interview, Sean Riley.
6. See www.meetlalo.com/blogs/news/lalos-the-chair-is-the-best-high-chair-and-heres-why.

Chapter 4

1. https://www.uclahealth.org/news/article/daily-aspirin-no-longer-recommended-to-prevent-heart-disease.
2. See www.cokesolutions.com/products/articles/coca-cola-life-gains-a-life-of-its-own.html.
3. See www.entrepreneur.com/franchises/the-king-of-smoothie-king-how-an-unlikely-franchisee-from/435856#:~:text=Wan.
4. See www.entrepreneur.com/franchises/how-the-ceo-of-smoothie-king-went-from-small-business-owner/298162.
5. See www.forbes.com/sites/simonmainwaring/2020/05/05/purpose-at-work-how-smoothie-king-drives-impact-through-international-franchises/.

Chapter 5

1. See www.qsrmagazine.com/story/top-50-fast-food-chains-ranked-2024/.
2. See https://adage.com/article/marketing-news-strategy/southwest-baggage-policy-change-social-post-draws-backlash/2605541.
3. See https://adage.com/article/marketing-news-strategy/southwest-baggage-policy-change-social-post-draws-backlash/2605541.
4. See www.salesforce.com/news/stories/the-history-of-salesforce/.
5. See www.theautochannel.com/news/press/date/20000615/press018285.html.
6. See https://martinroll.com/resources/articles/strategy/uniqlo-the-strategy-behind-the-global-japanese-fast-fashion-retail-brand/#.
7. See www.nytimes.com/2024/10/17/style/clare-waight-keller-uniqlo-givenchy.html?smid=nytcore-ios-share&referringSource=articleShare.

Chapter 6

1. See https://www.cnbc.com/2018/11/01/halo-top-beat-ben--jerrys-brings-in-hundreds-of-millions-in-sales.html.
2. See www.bloomberg.com/news/features/2024-09-13/nike-nke-stock-upheaval-defines-ceo-john-donahoe-s-tenure.

3. See https://www.worldfootwear.com/news/deckers-announces-full-year-results/8874.html.
4. See https://ir.deckers.com/news-events/press-releases/press-release/2024/DECKERS-BRANDS-REPORTS-FOURTH-QUARTER-AND-FULL-FISCAL-YEAR-2024-FINANCIAL-RESULTS/.
5. See https://blog.finishline.com/the-history-of-on-running/.
6. See https://hypebeast.com/2025/3/on-running-2024-revenue-beats-forecast-2025-growth-on-holding-ag-info.
7. See www.mastershoe.co.uk/oofos_history.
8. See www.oofos.com/blogs/ooah-moments/exos-x-oofos-vice-president-of-performance-brent-callaway-drives-athletic-achievement-via-active-recovery.
9. See www.ft.com/content/5ca1c4e1-2083-4525-b85f-0ae7c28cb690.
10. See www.latimes.com/business/story/2024-05-07/kim-kardashian-skims.
11. See https://www.ft.com/content/5ca1c4e1-2083-4525-b85f-0ae7c28cb690.
12. See www.wsj.com/style/fashion/a-hit-brands-one-size-fits-most-clothing-is-dividing-americas-teens-c6da9cc0.
13. See www.expressnews.com/sa-inc/article/alvaro-aguilar-hamburgers-cuarto-de-kilo-19387817.php.
14. See https://t2t.org/our-impact/.
15. See www.charitywatch.org/charities/stephen-siller-tunnel-to-towers-foundation.
16. See www.strollmag.com/locations/historic-brookhaven-ga/articles/-6dd257/.
17. See www.youtube.com/watch?v=66kgittqUwY.

Chapter 7

1. See www.bosshunting.com.au/style/accessories/history-of-rimowa/.
2. See www.rimowa.com/us/en/heritage.
3. See www.adsoftheworld.com/campaigns/engineered-for-life.
4. See www.tumi.com/about.
5. See www.cnbc.com/2016/03/03/samsonite-to-buy-tumi-for-18-billion-in-its-largest-deal-since-2011.html.
6. See www.prnewswire.com/il/news-releases/introducing-tumi-experience-collector-302230657.html.

7. See www.businessofbusiness.com/articles/history-of-away-luggage-data/.
8. See https://craftberry.co/articles/reinventing-e-commerce-the-history-of-shopify-2004-2024.
9. See www.ft.com/content/0ac81261-0e03-4d2e-bbe8-4fda21b8d1ad.
10. See www.shopify.com/blog.
11. See www.businessofapps.com/data/airbnb-statistics/#:~:text=CNBC%2C%20Company%20data-,Airbnb%20Listings,a%20new%20record%20for%20Airbnb.
12. See www.searchlogistics.com/learn/statistics/airbnb-statistics/.
13. See www.budgetyourtrip.com/hotels/united-states-of-america-US.
14. See https://teams-blog.operto.com/history-of-vrbo-vacation-rental-by-owner/.
15. See www.usatoday.com/story/sports/ncaaf/sec/2024/09/05/nick-saban-vrbo-commercial-daddy-time/75044805007/.
16. See www.businessinsider.com/airbnb-calls-vrbo-desperate-for-billboard-about-hosts-ad-campaign-2025-3.
17. See www.bizjournals.com/seattle/stories/2000/08/21/daily9.html.
18. See https://medium.com/@tinaphm7/online-reflection-week-14-human-centred-design-a827bccf375e.
19. See https://interbrand.com/best-global-brands/.
20. See https://hbsp.harvard.edu/product/W19666-PDF-ENG.
21. See https://digitalmag.theceomagazine.com/rise-of-the-decacorn/?r=global.
22. See www.businessofapps.com/data/most-popular-apps/.
23. See www.advisorperspectives.com/articles/2025/02/22/tiktok-owner-bytedance-tech-darling-400-billion-valuation.
24. See www.scmp.com/business/china-evs/article/3301358/tesla-sales-slump-china-buyers-turn-domestic-rivals-xpeng-byd-xiaomi.
25. See www.scmp.com/business/china-evs/article/3301358/tesla-sales-slump-china-buyers-turn-domestic-rivals-xpeng-byd-xiaomi.
26. See www.cnet.com/home/electric-vehicles/xiaomis-striking-su7-ultra-on-track-to-be-a-global-ev-success/.
27. See https://www.mi.com/global/discover/article?id=3879.

28. See www.businesswire.com/news/home/20200427005378/en/Xpeng-P7-Launches-in-China.
29. See https://www.forbes.com/sites/ywang/2024/03/04/elon-musk-failed-to-quash-this-chinese-billionaires-tesla-rival---now-its-going-global/.

Chapter 8

1. See www.nytimes.com/2009/12/17/business/media/17accenture.html.
2. See www.statista.com/statistics/272698/global-market-share-held-by-mobile-operating-systems-since-2009/#:~:text=Android%20maintained%20its%20position%20as,percent%20during%20the%20same%20period.
3. See www.nytimes.com/2013/10/13/magazine/who-made-that-android-logo.html.
4. See www.thestreet.com/technology/history-of-snapchat.
5. See www.emarketer.com/content/instacart-dominates-grocery-delivery-uber-doordash-catching-up.
6. See www.instacart.com/company/updates/carrot-evolution-a-new-brand-identity.
7. See https://woven.agency/insights/evolution-of-the-pepsi-logo/.
8. See www.forbes.com/sites/janelee/2012/10/02/deconstructing-the-tiffany-setting-the-worlds-most-popular-engagement-ring-style/.
9. See www.adweek.com/brand-marketing/how-tiffany-s-iconic-box-became-world-s-most-popular-package-160228/.
10. See www.adweek.com/brand-marketing/how-tiffany-s-iconic-box-became-world-s-most-popular-package-160228/.
11. See www.vogue.co.uk/article/christian-louboutin-painful-shoes-comfortable-shoes.
12. See www.mashed.com/630454/the-story-behind-crumbl-cookies-iconic-pink-box-exclusive/.
13. See www.mashed.com/630454/the-story-behind-crumbl-cookies-iconic-pink-box-exclusive/.
14. See https://adage.com/article/marketing-news-strategy/behind-graza-founder-andrew-benins-unorthodox-approach/2535281?utm_source=ad-age-don-t-%E2%80%A63/13.

15. See https://adage.com/article/marketing-news-strategy/behind-graza-founder-andrew-benins-unorthodox-approach/2535281?utm_source=ad-age-don-t-%E2%80%A63/13.
16. See www.forbes.com/sites/avidan/2013/02/26/constellation-transforms-the-wine-market-with-inside-the-box-thinking/.
17. See www.blackboxwines.com/why-black-box.html.
18. See https://wineindustryadvisor.com/2022/03/17/black-box-wines-introduces-savvy-man-national-media-campaign/.
19. See www.nytimes.com/2022/08/10/style/issey-miyake-steve-jobs-black-turtleneck.html.
20. See https://x.com/dnystedt/status/1664431370314342400.
21. See www.cnbc.com/2017/06/08/sap-ceo-bill-mcdermott-on-losing-an-eye-my-accident-changed-my-life-for-the-better.html.
22. See www.nbcnewyork.com/news/sen-john-fetterman-shorts-hoodie-sneakers-trump-inauguration/6114684/.

Chapter 9

1. See https://time.com/6964235/jensen-huang-2024/.
2. See www.acquired.fm/episodes/jensen-huang/.
3. See www.newyorker.com/magazine/2023/12/04/how-jensen-huangs-nvidia-is-powering-the-ai-revolution.
4. Tae Kim. *The Nvidia Way: Jensen Huang and the Making of a Tech Giant.* W.W. Norton & Company, 2024.
5. Tae Kim. *The Nvidia Way: Jensen Huang and the Making of a Tech Giant.* W.W. Norton & Company, 2024.
6. See https://archive.computerhistory.org/resources/access/text/2014/05/102746834-05-01-acc.pdf.
7. See https://engineering.stanford.edu/news/jen-hsun-huang-nvidia-co-founder-invests-next-generation-stanford-engineers.
8. See https://www.youtube.com/watch?v=9hzVdV63scU&t=787s, https://newsroom.haas.berkeley.edu/nvidia-ceo-jensen-huang-on-inventing-new-markets/.
9. See https://web.archive.org/web/19970213022030/http://www.orchid.com/products/righteous/r3d.html.

10. See www.newyorker.com/magazine/2023/12/04/how-jensen-huangs-nvidia-is-powering-the-ai-revolution.
11. Tae Kim. *The Nvidia Way: Jensen Huang and the Making of a Tech Giant*. W.W. Norton & Company, 2024.
12. Tae Kim. *The Nvidia Way: Jensen Huang and the Making of a Tech Giant*. W.W. Norton & Company, 2024.
13. See https://www.youtube.com/watch?v=H-BUvTomA7M.
14. See https://www.nytimes.com/2006/07/24/technology/24cnd-semi.html.
15. See www.newyorker.com/magazine/2023/12/04/how-jensen-huangs-nvidia-is-powering-the-ai-revolution.
16. See www.newyorker.com/magazine/2023/12/04/how-jensen-huangs-nvidia-is-powering-the-ai-revolution.
17. See https://www.thestreet.com/technology/nvidia-company-history-timeline.
18. See https://nvidianews.nvidia.com/news/nvidia-ceo-jensen-huang-and-industry-visionaries-to-unveil-whats-next-in-ai-at-gtc-2025.

Chapter 10

1. Interview, Sean Riley.
2. See www.usatoday.com/story/money/2024/12/20/nike-ceo-elliott-hill/77105986007/.
3. See www.cnbc.com/2024/10/31/starbucks-plan-to-return-to-its-roots-involves-200000-sharpies.html.
4. See www.today.com/food/restaurants/starbucks-discontinuing-drinks-rcna193083.
5. See www.wsj.com/business/retail/athletic-brewing-company-nonalcoholic-beer-valuation-a743d2d6.
6. See www.businesswire.com/news/home/20201118005330/en/International-Beer-Challenge-2020-Names-Athletic-Brewing-Company-North-American-Brewer-of-the-Year.
7. See www.wsj.com/business/retail/athletic-brewing-company-nonalcoholic-beer-valuation-a743d2d6.
8. See www.prnewswire.com/news-releases/one-of-nations-top-realtors-opens-independent-brokerage-mark-spain-real-estate-300213216.html.

9. See https://variety.com/2013/biz/news/epic-fail-how-blockbuster-could-have-owned-netflix-1200823443/.
10. See https://techcrunch.com/2012/03/30/netflix-sharpens-focus-on-dvds-with-dvd-com-but-dont-cry-qwikster-its-staying/.
11. See https://money.cnn.com/2011/10/10/technology/netflix_qwikster/?source=cnn_bin.
12. See www.theatlantic.com/technology/archive/2012/03/netflix-snaps-dvdcom-domain-its-dvd-holdouts/329896/.
13. See www.nytimes.com/2023/03/05/arts/television/chris-rock-netflix.html.

Chapter 11

1. See https://industrytoday.com/green-harvest/.
2. See www.nytimes.com/2022/01/19/business/laurel-cutler-dead.html.
3. See www.cnn.com/2022/07/13/business/gap-history-old-navy-retail/index.html.
4. See https://therobinreport.com/the-saga-of-gaps-decline-and-fall/.
5. See https://www.gapinc.com/en-us/articles/2025/03/gap-inc-reports-fourth-quarter-and-fiscal-2024-res
6. See https://www.theguardian.com/fashion/2022/apr/05/gap-how-the-clothing-brand-lost-its-way-fashion-retail.
7. See www.vogue.com/article/zac-posen-gap-profile-winter-2025.
8. See https://people.com/anne-hathaway-gap-gown-available-to-buy-8654727.
9. See https://www.adweek.com/brand-marketing/gaps-comeback-continues-with-troye-sivan-fronted-ode-to-denim/.
10. See www.fastcompany.com/91201578/gu-uniqlos-sister-store-what-to-know.
11. See https://adage.com/article/marketing-news-strategy/what-celsius-alani-nu-deal-means-beverage-marketing/2603321.
12. See https://adage.com/article/marketing-news-strategy/what-celsius-alani-nu-deal-means-beverage-marketing/2603321.
13. See www.washingtonpost.com/news/voraciously/wp/2019/09/10/the-key-to-white-claws-surging-popularity-marketing-to-a-post-gender-world/.
14. See www.youtube.com/watch?v=FApbkER3uIY.

Acknowledgments

I am forever grateful to the one and only Al Ries, without whom neither this book nor I would ever have happened.

In the beginning, he was just my dad. I was the only child from my father's second and forever marriage to Mary Lou Ries. While he was several years older than the other dads in the neighborhood, you would never have known it. His energy was boundless. He gave everything he had to his work, his clients, his family, and especially me. I was born the year before positioning got its big break with the series of articles in *Advertising Age*. So, I grew up alongside positioning. And my intro to marketing started at an early age.

We always watched *M*A*S*H* during dinner on a little TV with bunny ears in the kitchen. The show was great, but the real show was my dad during the commercials. He would do a running commentary reviewing each commercial and the brand strategies behind them. Most often the brands were making terrible errors, including line extension, using weak slogans, or having unmemorable visuals. He loved to teach. And he was amazing at it. He spoke to me and my mom like we were the CEOs of companies and could actually do something to fix these branding woes. He did his best night after night to persuade us.

Later as a teen, I would roll my eyes when these marketing 101 lessons were sparked, not because I didn't want to hear them, but by then I had been indoctrinated and usually could guess what he might say next: "You were in Denver and asked the bartender for a local beer. He said sure, we call it a 'Colorado Kool-Aid'. That was the big idea. Coors should have positioned itself as the pioneer in light beer. It was already known as a lighter beer; it was the original! It could have been the only brand that wasn't a line extension. Coors should be the leader today, not Bud Light or Miller Lite."

He would repeat the story in full to us often—not because he forgot he told us before but because he believed in the repetition of ideas. Never assume your position is firmly anchored in the mind; you need to keep repeating it so nobody will forget it. I will never forget his stories. They are the foundation of my marketing education and fueled my desire to tell my own stories in this book.

My dad loved to inspire others. He was incredibly gracious with his time, especially to anybody who sought out his opinion, and even those who didn't. He would call and write to companies and give them advice for their brands. His books were a manifestation of his desire to teach and inspire others. He wanted to make all companies great. People too—he mentored countless people besides me.

I was in middle school when I decided to read the book my dad had written a few years prior. I can remember it like it was yesterday, this sudden epiphany while reading the words. "OMG, my dad is amazing. This book is amazing. It's interesting and fun to read." The book had sold me hook, line, and sinker.

Before reading *Positioning*, I wanted to be an actress. After reading *Positioning*, I wanted to work with my dad. I never said it out loud. Nor did my dad. It was just an energy between us of what the future destiny would be. He didn't push it; I didn't ask. But he started sharing some fundamentals, and our partnership began.

His teaching skills were a big help at homework time. He had been a math major in college, and I loved math. But projects and presentations were where we both shined. We worked together as if we were in an ad agency—he was the account manager, and I was the assistant manager. He taught me how to clearly present ideas and how to visualize them. As early as elementary school, I had flip charts, posters, and even dragged a slide projector to a fifth-grade class presentation. The other kids looked at me weird, but I didn't care. I was practicing for my future.

As I got older and papers were assigned, my dad would give me the skills I needed to write this book. First, I would write a draft, which I am sure was horrible. He would never say that. Instead he said, "This is terrific, Laura. You are a great writer; it just needs some editing." Then he would sit with me for hours, scissors in hand, cutting up what I wrote and then helping me to organize and add connecting thoughts. Everything was Scotch taped onto new pieces of paper. Ideas could not be randomly blurted out on the page; they needed to connect to each other. The last sentence must "hook" to the next. This mantra was on loop in my mind while writing and editing this book.

When I finally got to work with my dad in 1994, it was magical. I was a sponge by his side watching the master at work. Our business partnership spanned almost 30 years. And I went from a marketing novice to his partner to leading the company.

My father was my hero, my teacher, my mentor, my partner, my friend, and always my dad. I have squeezed out all he taught me and all he empowered me to be to write this book. It also has a bit of my own spin. I wish he could read it. I am sure he would say it's terrific, and I know he would give me some tips. I miss him dearly.

Al Ries passed away peacefully October 7, 2022, a month shy of his 96th birthday.

About the Author

Laura Ries is a world-famous positioning consultant and best-selling author.

In 1994, Laura joined her father, Al Ries, the legendary positioning pioneer and co-author of the world's best-selling marketing book, *Positioning: The Battle for Your Mind*, to work in the company now known as RIES.

With Al, Laura is the co-author of five groundbreaking books that have taken part in reshaping modern marketing—including *The 22 Immutable Laws of Branding* and *The Fall of Advertising & The Rise of PR*. In addition, Laura is the author of *Visual Hammer*, which integrates visuals as a powerful new dimension in positioning strategy. Laura and Al's works have influenced minds, cementing their legacy as best-selling visionaries whose ideas continue to drive the global marketing debate.

Since 2022, Laura continues her father's legacy as Chairwoman of RIES, guiding the expansion and global influence of the leading positioning strategy and consulting firm with representation and offices in the United States, Europe, China, and South America.

With RIES, Laura has consulted and given advice to companies and entrepreneurs around the world on positioning strategy. She blends three decades of hands-on experience with deep strategic thinking. In her global consulting work Laura leads RIES expert teams to help clients deliberately choose a strategic enemy—whether it's another category, mindset, or status quo—to position their brands for clarity and to create a rallying point for business growth.

Beyond her consulting work, Laura is a sought-after speaker and has traveled to more than 60 countries teaching the fundamental principles of positioning, visual hammer, the immutable laws of branding, and the strategic enemy. She has appeared on major television channels such as CNBC, Fox News, Fox Business, ABC, NBC, and CNN as an expert providing insights on positioning, branding, and marketing strategies.

Learn more at RIES.com.

Index

Page numbers followed by *f* refer to figures.

Accenture, 126–127
Ace Hardware, 12–13
Adidas, 130
Advertising, 43–44, 164
Aflac, 39
Aguilar, Alvaro, 89, 90, 92, 94–95
Airbnb, 111–113
Air Jordan, 130
Alani Nu, 184
Amazon, 109–111, 116, 160
AMD, 158
American vs. Chinese brands, 116–123
Anchor, 160–161, 164–165
Android, 132
Anthony, Mike, 140
Apple, 21–23, 116, 131–132, 148
Aspirin, 47
Athletic Brewing Company, 169–170
ATI, 157–158
Atwood, Kate, 99–100
Away Luggage, 108, 109

Band-Aid, 24
Barilla, 164

Bayer, 47–48
Benin, Andrew, 140
Benioff, Marc, 70–72
Ben & Jerry's, 82
Bernhard, Olivier, 85
Bezos, Jeff, 161
BlackBerry, 22, 23
Black Box, 141–142
Blakely, Sara, 32
Blockbuster, 172
BlueChew, 78
BMW, 7, 122, 126
Boston Beer Company, 185–186
Boston Chicken, 9, 10
Boston Market, 9
Brand(s), xi, xii. *See also* Categories
   launching, 175–189
   multiple, 112 (*See also* Line extensions)
   of USA vs. China, 116–123
Branding/brand building, xii, 1
   narrow focus in, 40, 42
   public relations for, 156–157
   by saying no, 75–78

213

Brand names, 9–10, 46–47
Brandy Melville, 88–89
Brown, Reggie, 133
Buck, Ian, 158
Budweiser, 25, 51, 55–59
Bugaboo, 41
Burger King, 66, 67, 90, 135
BYD, 120–122
ByteDance, 117–119

Callie's Hot Little Biscuits, 111
Camp, Garrett, 32
Campbell's, 179–180
Carl's Jr., 90, 91
Carnegie, Dale, 46
Castellanos, Ricardo, 177
Categories, 15–28, 164–165
   and being your own enemy, 175–189
   consumers' changing of, 16–17
   consumers' verbalizing of, 24–28
   creating, 17–19
   defining, 195
   launching new, 60–61, 155, 176, 178
   names of, 19–23
   for Nvidia, 154–155
   as strategic enemy, 32–44
Cathy, S. Truett, 66
Celsius, 183–184
Cessario, Mike, 33–34
Charmin, 35, 47
Chevrolet, 47
Chick-fil-A, 66–67

China vs. American brands, 116–123
Chipotle, 59–60, 67
Choices, 3–5
Clearly Canadian, 20
Clifford, Charlie, 107
Clouse, David, 112
Coca-Cola, 11, 30, 47–53, 57, 126, 129, 130, 185, 191
Colgate, 30, 81, 139
Color, 131, 132, 136–139
Constellation Brands, 141–142
Coors, 20, 25–26, 55
Corona, 11, 56, 57, 126
Costco, 4
Cottonelle, 34
Crocs, 86
Crumbl Cookies, 138, 139
C2, 49
Cuarto de Kilo, 89–95, 90f, 91f
Cullen, Sara, 77
Cutler, Laurel, 179

Davidson, Carolyn, 130
Debates, 103–123
   engagement from, 104
   on the Internet, 104–105
   kicking off, 195
   lodging, 111–113
   luggage, 105–109
   online shopping, 109–111
   toothbrushes, 113–116
   USA vs. China, 116–123
Deckers Brands, 85
Deloitte, 126
Delta, 69

Difference, distinctiveness and, xii, 5–7. *See also* Visual hammer
Digital Equipment, 81
Dockers, 37–38
DocuSign, 24
Domino's, 67, 126
Donahoe, John, 83, 84
DoorDash, 134
Douyin, 118
Drexler, Mickey, 180, 182
Dude Wipes, 34, 35, 165–166
Dunkin' Donuts (Dunkin'), 8, 67
Duracell, 19
Dyson, 164

E. & J. Gallo, 142, 188
Edible Arrangements (Edible), 10
Emotions, 10–11, 127–128
Enemy:
    creating your own, 175–189
    strategic (*see* Strategic enemy(-ies))
    your core brand as (*see* Line extensions)
Ernst & Young, 126
Estes, Greg, 160
Eveready, 19
Expedia Group, 112–113

Facebook, 47, 133
Fairlife, 54
The Farmer's Dog, 27–28, 31
Fehrnstrom, Chris, 141–142
Ferrari, 126

Fetterman, John, 144
Fields, Debbie, 138, 139
Fisher, Don, 180
Fisher, Doris, 180
Focus, xii, 79–101
    on enemy of your brand, 59–62
    loss of, 80, 83–86
    narrow, 40, 42, 86–95, 176
    for nonprofits, 95–101
    for Nvidia, 148–151, 153–155, 159–160
    pivoting, 81–83
    visual hammer and battle cry for, 91–95, 91*f*
Franklin, Shirley, 145
Freshpet, 26–27
Frisbee, 24

Gablinger, 24
The Gap, 180–182
Gap Inc., 75, 180, 181
Garza, Miguel, 168
Garza, Veronica, 167–168
Gass, Nancy, 97
Gatorade, 3
GEM, 77–78
General Motors, 16–18, 80
Gilbert, Ben, 159
Gira-Grill, 89–90, 90*f*, 94, 95
Goldfish, 126
Google, 24, 47, 116, 132, 160
Graza, 139–141
Green Giant, 126
Greyhound, xii
GU, 182–183
Guiliani, David, 114

Haagen Dazs, 82
Halife, Johnny, 197
Halo Top, 81–83
Hastings, Reed, 172, 173
Heineken, 170
Hemsley, Sawyer, 138
He Xiaopeng, 122
High Noon, 188
Hill, Elliot, 83, 166
H&M, 75
Hoka, 84–85
Holmes, Elizabeth, 143
HomeAway, 112, 113
Honda, 116
Huang, Jensen, 121, 123, 143, 148–154, 158–161
Huawei, 116
Hutson, Robert, 115
Hyundai, 18

IBM, xi, 80
Instacart, 134–135
Instagram, 47, 133, 136
Intel, 80, 154
iPhone, 22–23, 32, 131
iPod, 22, 81, 131
Isadora, 178–179
Iyengar, Sheena, 4

Jack, Alex, 197
Jacuzzi, 24
Japanese products, 116–117
JetBlue, 126
Jobs, Steve, 22–23, 131, 143, 161
Jones, Harvey, 151–152
Jordan, Bob, 70

Kahneman, Daniel, 3
Kalanick, Travis, 32
Kardashian, Kim, 87
Kate's Club, 99–101
Kelleher, Herb, 68
Keller, Clare Waight, 75
KFC, 9, 88
Kim, Wan, 61
Kimball, Molly, 62
Kimberly-Clark, 35
KIND Bar, 77
Kit Kat, 7
Kleenex, 24, 34, 139
Kleiner Perkins, 150
Kmart, 31
Kodak, 38, 81, 176
Korey, Steph, 108
Krizhevsky, Alex, 159
Kuhnau, Steve, 60, 61

Lalo, 41–42
Land O'Lakes, Florida, 97
Leaders/leadership, 163–174
  to maintain focus, 159
  signature looks for, 143–145
  as strategic enemy, 30–31
Lei Jun, 120, 121
Lepper, Mark, 4
Levi Strauss, 37–38
Line extensions, 45–63, 176
  and brand name, 46–47
  brands weakened by, 83
  examples of, 47–59
  making decisions about, 59–62
  problems with, 46

Liquid Death, xii, 33–34
Logo, 130–135. *See also* Visual hammer
LongHorn Steakhouse, 126
Louboutin, 125, 137–138
Louboutin, Christian, 137
Lululemon, 38
Lutke, Tobias, 110
Lyft, 26

McDermott, Bill, 144
McDonald's, 11, 66, 67, 90, 125, 130
McGowan, Jason, 138
Macintosh, 132, 148
McNeil Laboratories, 48
Maev, 31
Malachowsky, Chris, 148, 149, 154
Mark Spain Real Estate, 170–172
Marlboro, 126
Marsan, Silvio, 88
Masters jackets, 125
Memory, 11–13, 128
Menards, 13
Mercedes, 130
Mercedes-Benz, 135
Message, 7–9, 11–13
Microsoft, xi, 116, 157, 160
Mike's Hard Lemonade, 56, 184–185
Miller Brewing Company, 24–25, 55, 56
Mind of the consumer, xi, 1–14
  and brand names, 9–10
  category folders in (*see* Categories)
  and distinctiveness, 5–7
  and emotions, 10–11
  and memory, 11–13
  and number of choices, 3–5
  and reality, 13
  and simplicity, 7–9
  understanding, 192–197
  words vs. visuals in, 126
Minute Maid, 51–53
Modelo Especial, 57
Molson Coors, 52
Monster, 6, 7, 47
Morszeck, Paul, 105–106
Morszeck, Richard, 106
Mrs. Fields, 138–139
Muller, George, 73
Mulvaney, Dylan, 57
Murphy, Bobby, 133
Murray, Ian, 38, 39
Murray, Shep, 38, 39
Musical.ly, 117–119
Musk, Elon, 17, 122

Name(s), 196
  brand, 9–10, 24, 46–47
  category, 19–24
  of Nvidia, 149–150, 161
  of visual hammers, 130
Netflix, 172–174
New Balance, 130
Newton, 21, 22
Niccol, Brian, 166–167
Nike, 7, 83–84, 130, 166
Nissan, 116
Nixta Taqueria, 168
Nokia, 22, 23

Nonprofits, 95–101
"No," saying, 65–78, 194
   existing brands' examples of, 65–75
   new brands built by, 75–78
   by Nvidia, 149–151
Nvidia, xi, 121, 123, 147–161
   focus of, 148–151, 153–155, 159–160
   funding for, 150–151
   and gaming graphics chips, 160–161
   and GPUs, 158–159
   and multimedia vs. graphics only, 151–152
   names used by, 149–150, 161
   public relations by, 156–157
   speed of development by, 153–154
   strategic enemies of, 152–154, 157–158
   visual hammer of, 161

Oatly, 53–55, 164
Obama, Barack, 22
Old Navy, 180–182
Olipop, 52, 53
On, 85–86
OOFOS, 86
Oracle, 71–72
Oral-B, 113–116

Pabst, Thomas, 156
Packaging, 139–142
Palm Computing, 22

Panda Dunks, 84
Panda Express, 67, 126
Panera Bread, 67
PepsiCo, 3, 30, 135, 168–169, 184
Perception, 13, 66
P&G, 35
Philips, 114–115
Photoshop, 24
Pizza Hut, 10, 135
Podojil, Emerson, 97–99
Polo, 36, 40–41
Poppi, 52, 53
Posen, Zac, 182
Positioning, xi, 192–193. *See also* Strategy(-ies)
   Huang on, 151–152
   and mind of the consumer, 1–2, 192–193
   strategic enemy for, 43–44
   verbal, 126
PowerBar, 75–77
P.R. Mallory Company, 19
Prego, 179–180
Priem, Curtis, 148–150
Puma, 130

Q-Tips, 24
Quest Bars, 76–77

Ralph Lauren, 36, 40–41
Randolph, Marc, 172
Reality, 13, 66
Red Bull, 6, 7, 183
Red Hat, 126

Reebok, 130
Rehbock, Bill, 156
Repetition, 11–13, 129
Riccobono, Chris, 35–36
Ries, Al, ix–x, 3, 19, 21, 23, 26, 44, 89, 92, 123, 165, 177, 178
Riley, Sean, 34, 165–166
Rimowa, 105–109
Rivian, 121
Ro (Roman Health Ventures), 78
Rock, Chris, 174
Rolex, 129
Rosales, Sergio, 176
Rubio, Jen, 108
RXBAR, 76–77

Saban, Nike, 113
Salesforce, xi, 30, 70–72
Samsonite, 107
Santayana, George, 49
Saturn, 16–17
Schwartz, Barry, 4
Scope, 30
Scott, 47
Sears, 80
Sellers, Scott, 151
Sequoia Capital, 150
Shein, 183
Shell, 126
Shields, Nick, 185
Shopify, 109–111
Shufelt, Bill, 169
Siete, 167–169
Signature looks, 143–145

Silicon Graphics, 152
Siller, Frank, 96
Siller, Stephen, 96
Simplicity, 7–9
Simply, 51–53
Sivan, Troye, 182
Skims, 86–87
Skittles, 8
Smalls, 28
Smasherson Foundation, 97–99
Smith, Ross, 152
Smoothie King, 60–62
Snapchat, 133
Snowdevil, 110
Sonicare, 113–116
Sony, 80, 117
Southwest Airlines, 68–70, 196–197
Southworks, 192–196
Spain, Mark, 170–172
Spanx, 32, 86–87
Spiegel, Evan, 133
SpikedSeltzer, 185–186
Stam, Nick, 156
Starbucks, 8, 50, 67, 164, 166–167, 196
Strategic enemy(-ies), xii, 29–44, 193–194
   debates among (*see* Debates)
   focusing on, 59–62
   value of, 2
Strategy(-ies), xi, 191–197
   and the brain, 128–129
   defining your category, 195
   kicking off debate, 195

Strategy(-ies) (*continued*)
   making changes, 196–197
   name and visual hammer, 196
   positioning message, 192–193
   saying no, 194
   strategic enemy, 193–194
   verbal, 126
Subaru, 72–73, 122
Subway, 67
Sun Microsystems, 149
Sutskever, Ilya, 159

Taco Bell, 67
Target, 8, 11, 30, 126, 129
Tesla, 17–18, 120–122, 164
3dfx, 152–153
Tide, 30
Tiffany, 30, 125, 136–137
Tiffany, Charles, 136, 137
TikTok, 117–119, 134
Tommy John, 8
Toyota, 47, 116
Trademarks, 126–127
Triscuits, 5–6
Tropicana, 11, 30, 51–52
Trout, Jack, ix, 44
Tumi, 107
Tunnel to Towers Foundation, 96–97
Twisted Tea, 56
Tylenol, 48

Uber, 24, 26, 32–33
Uber Eats, 134

Under Armour, 130
Uniqlo (Unique Clothing Warehouse), 74–75, 182
USA vs. China debate, 116–123
UNTUCKit, 35–37

Verde Valle, 176–179
Vineyard Vines, 38–40
Visuals, 10–11, 126–129
Visual hammer, xii, 125–145, 196
   changing your, 135–136
   for fashion brands, 36
   logo as, 130–135
   naming, 130
   of Nvidia, 161
   packaging as, 139–142
   power and benefits of, 127–129
   signature looks as, 143–145
   singular color for, 136–139
   trademarks vs., 126–127
   for your focus, 91–95, 91*f*
Vivoli, Dan, 155, 156, 158
Vlad, Oana, 48–49
Vodoo Graphics, 152–153
Volkswagen, 91
Volvo, 46, 122
Von Mandl, Anthony, 185
VRBO (Vrbo), 112–113

Walker, John, 169
Wallace, Trevor, 187
Wal-Mart, 4, 30
Wells Enterprises, 83

Wendy's, 67
White Claw, 56, 184–188
Wintour, Anna, 145
Woods, Tiger, 126–127
Woolverton, Justin, 81
Wybo, German Rosales, 179

Xerox, 24, 46–47
Xiaomi, 116, 119–121
XPeng, 121–123

Yahoo, 47
Yanai, Tadashi, 74, 75
Young Men's Service League, 43–43
YouTube, 47, 119

Zara, 74, 75
Zhang Yiming, 118
Zima, 20–21
Zuckerberg, Mark, 148, 161